Staying Me

Patrick McGail

First Edition

ISBN:1535131683
ISBN-13:978-1535131681

DEDICATION

I would like to dedicate this book to my loving parents who stand by me always.

I love you.

CONTENTS

ACKNOWLEDGMENTS

To my parents who love and support me; my brother, Alec, who encourages even my strangest ideas; to my sister, Autumn, who shows me true strength.

To Mark Senter, Jean Mullins, Jennifer Hansen, Ariana Barnhart, Kimberly Hogan, Diane Mengos, David Berger, Walker, Cole Rench, Savannah Hutchins, Father Jim Duell and all of my friends who continue to write and support me, my loving family who give me undying support even though they may be many miles away.

To Roy, Austin, Dave, Patrick, Kyle, DC, White, Trey, B, West, Walt, Joker, Maxie, Jason, Amigo, Jersey, Bo, Rose, Chris, Michael, Vegas, Sleepy, Lynn, Vampire, Quinn, Will, Joe, Free, Body, Rome and all of my friends who have given me support and encouragement in prison.

To the Miami County sheriffs who respected me and treated me with dignity.

And especially to my best friend Kevin without whom I would have been insane long ago.

And to all of you readers for supporting my message.

Thank you.

Prologue

One hundred and eighty five days ago I was sentenced to twenty four years to life for aggravated burglary, aggravated robbery, Murder and a gun specification. In my served time thus far I have been beaten, cheated, robbed, pressed for money and degraded. I have also read around one million nine hundred and seventy nine thousand two hundred and forty words, wrote approximately fifty seven thousand words of this book and five thousand of compiled other works, learned five hundred French words and phrases, made around four hundred and sixty phone calls, sent over a hundred digital messages, over fifty letters and have successfully not received a single tattoo. When charged with this crime I pleaded not guilty, a plea I have sustained since. This book is an anthology of my life in the prison system from my wrongful prosecution to the end of my district appeal process. Sitting in my cell alone as I write this preamble to my epic I can only imagine how it ends considering I have not yet felt the warmth of victory or the sting of defeat. Statistically speaking there is a good chance that this book is never published. However, if it is, I present a challenge to the reader. Question everything. When you see a conviction on the news question it. When you hear of injustice, stop it. When an innocent man is killed by the police, defend him. Don't allow the innocent to be judged based on the inadequacies of the guilty. Free men see the looming barbwire empires we slaves live in as monuments to derelict societies. Rather, question how many are innocent, how many have been residual or collateral damage of the judicial monster crushing so many. Stand up for what is right; hope, empathy, integrity and the ineffable human spirit that lies in so many of us here in blue, protected from this disgusting world in which we live. In several weeks I will be nineteen. Two years ago today I was preparing to graduate high school and start college. Two years ago I would drive to Indiana to visit my brother at his college. Two years ago I would hike, climb, run and celebrate my incredible future. Two years ago I had two friends who set on committing a terrible crime. Two years ago the first dominos fell that led me to cell 1A-229 in Warren Correctional Institution. Two years ago I visited Spain and Portugal. Two years ago I was sixteen. Two years ago I was happy. When you reader take to reading my odyssey of how this all ends you will get to know me. You will learn more about me than most people who consider themselves my closest friends know. And the final chapters are for now a mystery to both of us. But soon we will both know how it turns out. If you have a keen memory of current events you will likely know even more than I do know how this ends. If not, well then, you may be just as excited as I am to discover my fate. Without further ado I will take you back to the last day of my trial and the end of the beginning which is the beginning of the journey that I am approaching the end of now.

Intake

"Mr. McGail, you have been found guilty by this jury of murder, aggravated robbery and aggravated burglary. You will have a sentencing hearing September 26th and until that time you will be put into the custody of the sheriff."

The accumulated gasp could have sucked the room desolate of air. The sheriff walked the length of the circular court room.

"Get up."

My lawyer, Antonio, whispered in my ear. I stood up with muffled sobs coming from behind me and my lawyer's face going red with anger and shock. I stepped out from my chair and with the metallic clicks of the cold steel on my skin I was led by the juror's box. I looked first at the juror's box where not one of the men or woman offered so much as a glance and two of the women were crying silently and then the section of the audience reserved for the victims' family where I received the same. The door closed behind me and all at once it was silent.

"Step over here."

The sheriff ushered me toward a grey locker next to which was a steel door that the sheriff opened with one of a series of large keys.

"Step inside."

He seemed to be on edge as I scooted past him.

"Keep doing what you are doing and you will have nothing to worry about"

His voice seemed far away as if the volume had been turned down substantially. I stepped into a small cell and his voice faded as he closed the steel door behind me. Ahead was a barred gate followed by a long empty hallway. Much like the hallway my mind was blank. What had happened was hardly believable. I felt as though I was dreaming and would soon wake up several hours earlier. How could this happen? I just didn't....

Click!

I had not noticed the two correction officers walking down the long hallway. They opened the door with another of the large keys and directed me to walk forward. With each step I fell further and further into myself. My hearing became muffled and my eyes might have well been blind. My body was moving on autopilot. I was in the hallway. I was in an elevator (the light reading "one" was lit) and then I was in another hallway and finally I was alone in a room. The room was 10 feet long by 6 feet. It had a steel toilet and a mat laying on a stone altar. I sat on the bed and, still catatonic, began to finally wake up. I became aware of the writing on the wall, the hazy fluorescent light, the stale piss smell. The door clicked and opened.

"McGail, come out."

I eased off my bed and walked toward the large CO. He walked with me to a green pad on the wall.

"Put your head on the wall." I did as he said and he began to pat me down.

"Do you have any weapons on you?"

"No Sir." I said.

He reached in my pockets and turned them inside out.

"Take off your sweater, now your tie and shoes. Take off your socks... whoa, don't fall over... take off your button up shirt. Now follow me."

I followed him into a room with hundreds of square lockers. Each with a combination lock. He dropped the large black bag containing my clothes.

"Take off the rest of your clothes and drop them in this bag."

When all of my clothes were laying in the bag he pointed toward a small white walled shower next to another steel toilet by the door.

"Take a quick shower and put on the clothes on the bench."

I stepped inside and turned the shining knob. The water washed away some of the shock and into me more and more what was happening. As reality began to set in so did an aching fear. My eyes began to go out of focus with wave after wave of blinding fear. And then I was angry. This just didn't make sense. The guilty are guilty and the innocent go free. That was how it was supposed to be. How could they find me guilty of a crime I didn't---

"Time! dry off and get dressed."

I didn't have time to use soap but I turned off the water regardless and got dressed into the orange pants, shirt and flip flops

"Do I get underwear or socks?"

"You can buy socks from the commissary for $1.39 or a pair of underwear for $6.90."

"Oh...I'm okay."

He walked me back to my small cell and closed the door. Once again I sat upon my mat. From outside my door I could hear a drunkard ending his night unfavorably. Inside my cell I was trying to wrap my mind around how/why this happened. People say everything happens for a reason, that everything you go through just makes you stronger. But, I just couldn't wrap my mind around it. The slot halfway down my door opened and a voice came in from the other side.

"Cup!" I stood baffled.

"I'm sorry?" I knelt down and peered out the slot.

"Give me your cup."

"Oh, okay." I slid the stout brown cup out my slot. It was put back on the ledge with a light green liquid. I picked it up and right away a thick brown tray slid in the slot with two bologna sandwiches, a small amount of tortilla chips, a square "cake" that was much like a sponge cake with vanilla icing on its top and a scoop of mustard. I placed the cup on the sink that sat on my bed with the meal. I peeled the bologna off the sandwiches and laid it on the tray. I figured that since I haven't eaten meat in a year and half, why should I start now? I ate the two cheese sandwiches, the chips and the cake and slid the tray back into the slot I took it from. Then I picked up the juice and gave it an apprehensive taste. It was lime Kool-Aid. I drank it down and replaced the cup on top of the sink. I sat back down and reclaimed my pensive state and waited for something to happen. Minutes dragged on and still nothing happened. I paced around the small room wanting something, anything to happen. I thought about where I would be if they recognized my innocence. Celebrating with my family, jubilantly eating while praising my lawyer and his team for saving me from those terrible accusations and the subsequent life that they would lead. I just didn't understand what had happened. I laid down; stood up; laid down; sat up, paced around the room; tried to sing Fleet Foxes, Bon Iver and Modest Mouse songs to pass the time and get my mind off what was happening. I tried to do pushups. I tried to sleep. Nothing worked. Finally, and after what felt like an hour the tray moved out of the slot. I shot to the door and pressed my face in the slot.

"Can I make a phone call?" I blurted out to the CO's back.

"Yeah, just give me a minute to finish passing out trays."

"Thank you." I called back and laid on my mat relieved that at least I can talk to my parents.

Again, trapped in my own unease I made my rotations of laying down, standing up , sitting down, standing up, singing more songs by the Black Keys, Flaming Lips and more Bon Iver. Finally during a period of singing a song by Jimmy Buffet my door opened.

"McGail, come out." I jumped into my Bob Barker flip flops and walked out. "Please sit on the bench." I sat down next to a computer and he began to ask a series of questions.

"What is your height?"

"6 foot 1 inches."

"What is your weight?"

"155."

"Skin color?"

"...White."

"Eye color?"

"Brown."

"Hair Color?"

"Brown."

"Gang affiliation?"

"Umm...no."

"Alias?"

"Uhhh...Pat."

"Do you have bedbugs?"

"No"

"Do you drink alcohol?"

"No."

"Do you smoke tobacco?"

"Only as of recently."

"Do you use any illegal narcotics?"

"I've smoked a little marijuana."

"How much is a little?"

"Once or twice every couple of weeks."

"Okay, follow me." I followed him into a room with no door approximately 6 feet by 6 feet in diameter. It had a counter with a computer and a football helmet on it and a black chair used to restrain inmates. "Stand on the blue X on the floor." He indicated two small pieces of tape on the floor. I stood on the 'X' and noticed that directly ahead of me was a digital camera. "Stay still." I stood still and he walked out of the room. After a moment I heard him call "Turn to your right." I turned to my right and after another moment. "Turn to the left!" I turned to my left and waited. "Pull up you left sleeve and turn back to your right." I turned to my right and exposed my arm revealing my tattoo. "Now lift your right pant leg and face forward." I exposed the tattoo on my leg and waited a moment. "Now pull down your shirt so we can photograph the tattoo on your chest." I faced forward and waited a moment with my chest exposed. He returned and began walking me back to my cell.

"Can I make a phone call?"

"Oh...Yes." He turned us around and walked us into a room with two metal chairs in each corner and two phones on the wall, one silver , and one blue. He picked up the silver phone and after pressing a few digits he handed me the phone. Pausing; "Can you read?"

"Yes, ha-ha."

"Well you never know. Read the wall in front of you." When I finished he told me to hang up the phone. "Now hang on while I set you up." He left the room and I looked through the window in the door to the room with the lockers. I wondered how many of them were filled. How many people were kept here while the police hunted for more and the people slept soundly knowing the lockers were full. He came back in and pointed toward the phone.

"Your pin number is 76671." I picked up the phone and was immediately greeted by a female voice.

"For English, press or say one. Para Espanol, presione dos."

"One."

"For a collect call press or say one, for a calling card press or say two."

"One."

"Please enter or say your pin number now."

"7-6-6-7-1."

"This call is subject to recording and is monitored; you may hear silence during the acceptance of your call. Please continue to hold."

I didn't realize elevator music was still a prevalent thing on phone calls. For that matter I wondered who wrote these songs. Are there bands that exclusively---

"Thank you for using Securus, you may start the conversation now."

"Mom?"

My Mom responded. "Hey! Dad's here too. I'll put you on speaker."

"OK."

"Can you hear me?"

"Yes."

"Hey!"

"Hey guys, what's up?"

"Not a whole lot, still pretty much in shock."

"I know, I don't get it."

"Well Antonio is coming tomorrow to talk to you, he has some good news."

"Ok, awesome. I miss you guys."

" We miss you too. We love you."

" I love you guys too."

" Hang in there buddy. This is just one more step."

"Ok, I just---"

Just that quick the phone cut off with a click and the familiar woman's voice.

"Thank you for using Securus, goodbye." I stood in the small room alone and silent and I could feel the distance already. It hadn't struck me yet when I had walked through crash gates and been stripped of my freedom but with the phone going silent I knew it was real. At least they sounded happy. And they said Antonio had some good news so maybe I wouldn't have to stay for too long. I walked back out into the hallway and walked back toward my holding cell. The CO followed me and closed the door behind me. I laid down on the mat and wondered what my family was doing right now. They really did sound happy considering everything that happened. How could this all happen? How can your life be altered so quickly? I should have stopped them. I should have stopped them going in the house that night. I should have known… I slipped into sleep and when I awoke the lights were still on.

"Damn," I mumbled "it must still be early." I paced my cell and tried to understand how all of this could have happened. I laid back down on the mat and kept myself awake.

Isolation

I awoke again to the lights still on. I stood up and paced the cell. One... two... three... turn. I repeated over and over again. One... two... three... one... two... three... one... two... three... how long had I been there, 2 hours? I only had one meal so it couldn't have been more than that. Yet I had awoke twice so it could be that I missed a meal. I pressed my ear against the door and slid to the ground. I could hear the CO's move around outside the door to the other holding cells, the elevator, the control room and the Sally port which I surmised to be a garage to the right of my door. I kept my ear to the door to try to make a mental image of my bourgeois dungeon. My memory of the layout was hazy but after three hours (Judged by the six officer checks) I found there to be six holding cells, three on each side of the hallway. The Sally port was five paces to my right with a steel cage blocking the door. To the left of my cell there was a holding cell for suicidal isolation. Three paces past that cell there was a "T" in the hallway with the hallway to the left leading to the elevator and the hallway to the right leading to the room with the lockers on the left and the phone room and intake picture room on the left. Directly across from my cell there were three holding cells in a line. The cell in the middle had an assailant woman from the country, the right had a young shoplifter from the north side of town and the left had a belligerent man screaming about just what he would do if he got his hands on the extremity suckling monkey man that put him there. I had no neighbor to my right but to my left was a girl in the suicidal isolation cell. According to the correctional officers she was cutting herself with everything she could get a hold of, ripping her own hair out and attempting to poison herself with urine. The second floor must not have missed her much.

Hours stretched into eternity, not only did I know how many CO's there were, two, but I knew that one took quick strides evident of the shorter height while the other cleared the twenty feet from the elevator to the control room in just 8 strides, no doubt taller. I slipped into sleep with my head pressed against the door. When I woke up the door was open. I caught myself just before hitting the ground. The taller CO was standing above me.

"Do you want a shower?"

I squinted up at him "What time is it?"

"Midnight."

I sat up and walked back over to my altar and laid down. The door shut and I soon fell asleep. The next thirty six hours was more of the same. Sitting in the holding cell, slowly sliding into a ritual of listening to the new intakes, gossip from the COs, taking into account all of the COs, where their shifts brought them, who they were, etc... There was the large man who always worked in the control, the fat woman who walked through the whole building (I gauged the floors they went to by listening to the elevator), the skinny man on the floors one and three, the large gay man who worked nights, the seemingly mentally handicapped man who worked nights and the uptight - seemingly in charge man with military crisp strides.

By the third day I was allowed to go to the library. A hole in the third floor wall that contained love novels with saucy pages ripped out, a large collection of moth-eaten bibles and hidden deep in the stacks were books hoarded by patrons waiting to come back and claim their prizes. I returned to my cell just in time to be notified about a visitor. I imagined it must be my attorney. I walked with the Co to a room near the elevator with huge glass windows and a half basketball court connected. My attorney's assistant was sitting in a chair in the center of the room with another facing opposite. I sat down in the vacant chair and we spoke. It was brief and now I have trouble recalling what all was said. He told me that we would meet again, that family members of the victim's family were in the jail and to stay out of general population until everything was sorted out. Just as quickly as the conversation began it was done. He wasn't upset, not yet anyway. He was brimming with confidence of acquittal even still and walking out of the room I could see his effervescent smile.

The first day I started slow with *Hitchhikers Guide to the Galaxy* and *The Order of the Phoenix*. By the next day I was done but fortunately my parents had begun to bring books to the jail for me. The next three days I hardly ate, I slept in fleeting time when I couldn't bear to keep my eyes open any longer. In all other times I was completely immersed in the literary worlds of *Breakfast at Tiffany*, *House of Leaves*, *Bulfinch's Mythology*, *To Kill a Mockingbird*, *Candide*, *The Poems of Emily Dickinson*, *The Good Earth* and *Society and Its Discontents*. Granted, now with those days feeling like the beginning of a journey I took oh so long ago I cannot remember which of those books I read in that sadistic cell of eternal light or pressed in with the wolves. Ah, yes within those precise three days I was traveling under the direction of Messieurs, Truant and Zampano through the Navidson House. The rest of my reading spread throughout my stay there at Miami County Jail. On the morning of the sixth day my door was opened and I was told to collect my belongings and follow the portly woman. Standing in the elevator, traveling to general population the words of my lawyers associate, an estranged man plagued by delusions and substance abuse who later admitted to being mentally debilitated during the trial. He had told me to stay out of general population at all costs. I turned toward the woman and spoke.

"Can I stay in my holding cell?"

She turned and curtly shook her head. "No."

The elevator rang out and we began walking down the third floor hallway. Steel doors ran down the right and left sides of the hall. I racked my brain for everything I had heard. Everything I had learned and then it clicked.

"Don't you have to put me on suicide watch if I'm suicidal?"

She stopped and stared at me. "Are you going to be suicidal?"

I could feel the comfort of my cell again. "Yes."

She turned and we walked back to the elevator. Proud of myself I led the way out and to my cell. I stood there and the CO, coming around the corner, smiled.

"Oh, no, no, no." She led me to the cell next to mine and opened the door. It was 7X7 with a drain in the center and a camera toward the ceiling. There was no bed, toilet or sink. She handed me a large thick poncho and signaled toward the room. "Take off all your clothes, put this on and put your clothes out through the slot. You will have a psychological analysis in 24 hours to determine if you are truly a risk. The door closed and didn't open again for 24 hours. Until then I sat on the urine smelling floor naked save for the dress. I slept in spurts of ten minutes, unable to sleep anymore because of the smell.

After 24 hours I was led out of my seventh day of isolation and 24 hours of punishment for a mental dilemma into a large open room with two chairs and windows on the far side. There was a man sitting in one of the chairs and he smiled as I walked over.

"How are you doing?" I noticed his nose twitch at the smell of urine. "I see here you told the corrections officer that you want to hurt yourself?" My hair was matted on one side from the floor. I pulled a foreign hair from my arm with a foreign scab attached to it. He leaned forward. "C'mon, why would you want to do something like that?"

I shrugged.

"How long are you here for?"

"I don't know, yet." He took a note on his notepad.

"You're a young guy. What did you do?" I looked off out the windows to the sunshine. "Come on, man,. I don't watch the news, tell me."

"Why would I be on the news?" He took another note on his notepad. "I'm innocent and nobody believed me."

He sighed. "Well you know the system doesn't usually falter that bad." I looked at him for a long moment. He smiled back at me.

"Hey, catch the game Sunday?" My eyes narrowed.

"No, there's no TV in isolation."

He chuckled. "Of course, of course. Don't worry you didn't miss much." He wrote on his notepad. "Well, I would have to deem you a threat. You can return to your cell."

I stood up and walked back out the door. Just before reaching my cell I heard the CO talking to him about a follow-up check-up. Back in the suicide cell I paced barefoot on the sticky floor. In the blinding florescent sun I walked back and forth, back and forth. One, two, three, four, turn. One, two, three, four, turn. When I sat down the strong urine smell filled my nostrils so I stood as long as I could. After twenty eight thousand, eight hundred and twenty seven steps the door opened and in walked a crew cut, thin man with a virile smile and what I imagined to be adult onset homoerotic ideas. He stated, quite clearly that he knew for a fact that I was not suicidal and should tell him so. I retorted by stating that my self-harm was conditional to being placed with other prisoners. Assuming I could return to a single man cell I would happily declare myself not suicidal. With a thin smile he shrewdly let me know that the only places I would be allowed to occupy would be the "Piss hole" or general population. There would certainly be no exceptions, no in between and no alternative. I sat down and asked him kindly to leave.

"Excuse me, do you know who I am?" he hissed.

I was sure I didn't care. I sat looking straight ahead until he showed himself out of my studio toilet. With that, he left. Shortly thereafter I received my Kool-Aid, tortilla chips, bologna and cake. After my feast I paced the cell once again, three hours later my door opened again raining light into my incandescent cavern. I walked out, again barefoot and reeking of the stale film of filth from the floor. I was let into a room with two chairs again to meet my lawyers associate, Perry. I can't remember much from that encounter. He cried and apologized. He knew I didn't belong there and vowed to make it right. I cried as well, though only because of the estimated year it would take to get me out. Looking back as I write this a year isn't so long. But I suppose I knew even then what would happen. I also knew I had to go through a lot before it was over, and I had expected the trial to be the end. At the end of the meeting we hugged goodbye. I never saw him again.

I walked back to the small cell I inhabited and immediately upon entering the room fell upon my knees and threw up in the drain in the center of the room from the smell. I toppled to my side and coughed several times before coming to rest. Seconds later two separate things happened all at once. The drain was flushed just like a toilet for the first time in two days and my cell door opened.

"Come on out." I stood up wondering if my attorney had something he forgot to tell me. Instead I noticed it was two hours earlier. After lying down I had slept twenty hours, well into the next morning. I had been in the cell deemed the "Piss hole" for three days and two nights. I was led sheepishly into the room where I had made my phone calls to find a nice woman sitting in one of the chairs. I sat down opposite her and was appalled by the reflection of my face in the door window. My eyes had sunken, my hair was matted, tangled and dirty, my neck had a deep line in it from the suicide dress and I could clearly tell how much I stunk. Her name was Celeste and she spoke in an angelic harmony that reassured even the most pervasive concern. She was there to talk to me about how I felt. She was appalled by how the man a day ago had treated me. For the most part we didn't even talk about why I was in that room. We talked about her education and my education, interesting patients she had assessed, and why I wouldn't go into general population. She was sympathetic, she was professional, she was kind, she was the only sliver of humanity I would meet there and the only compassionate soul I would meet for quite some time after. When I left we shook hands and she told me she would try to keep me out of general population and tell the corrections officers I was not suicidal. I thanked her and walked back to my cell awaiting the verdict on where I would be going.

Genpop

Again I walked down the hallway leading to my new home. The air was cool, chilled by the cement and steel doors running the length of the hallway. From behind each steel gateway the sounds of justice reverberated. The low beat of televised urban music, laughter, anger, silence. This was our stop. The final door still stood guard over my belongings. I took up the mat, cup and spoon I had left days before. The large key sliding into its place. Every tumbler fit into the grooves. When he turned the metal it echoed throughout the halls of justice. The room, my foreseeable home, was a cage on three of its walls. On the outside of the cage was a catwalk for the correction officers to walk. We entered through one of the two doors leading to the catwalk. Walking down the catwalk I looked over my shoulder to the pod. I saw glances back at me from their beds. After severing my gaze they shared their own and began standing up, preparing to accept a new comer into the tribe of orange and blue. We stopped halfway down the first cage wall. A door stood in the bars and I then noticed that the cage was separated into two halves by a barred wall. When I walked through the first door I was standing in a small square *foyer*, five feet wide and five feet deep. The barred room connected the two sides of the cage with sliding barred doors and a barred door that served as their, our, exit. Entering the cage, the right door led to the sleeping area. The area had ten metal bunkbeds. On the wall near the cage was a steel toilet and sink where I would presumably be going to the bathroom. The bunks had occupants. The remaining open top racks were: the top rack to my left closest to the toilet, covered in books and two clear plastic totes. The one next to it was occupied by three strangers. The two top racks running against the cage to my right were open as well, so I took the one immediately to my right. The man on the bottom was a two hundred pound beer belly with several smudged tattoos on his arms. I walked up and nodded at the open rack. He stood up and took down several books and his tooth brush. I slung my mat up onto the rack and unfolded it so that the molded bloated 'head' section was toward the door. I positioned myself at one far end of the rack and swung onto the bed. Anchored into the cement floor the bunkbed didn't give the slightest bit with my assent. Perched atop my bed I watched the other inhabitants stand up and move about the pod.

One, the bottom rack closest to the toilet sat up and asked promptly, "Whatcha here for?"

This was it. This was the first moment of my stay where my first impression would define my stay and how comfortable I would be. My first words would need to be firm. Definite. A little intimidating.

"Hey, what is it? F-3? F-2? You're in orange, so I know you're not misdemeanor." I clenched my gut.

"Three, sorry, four F-1" the bottom rack on the far corner flanked by two walls looked up.

Toilet Rack spoke up again. "Jesus and- what was it?"

I did it. I made the right impression.

"Aggravated burglary, Aggravated robbery, murder and a gun specification."

Toilet Rack laughed "damn man, I guess you're not going to the IF."

I backtracked "Don't worry, I didn't do it."

He shook his head. "I'm not worried. Say, were you on the news?"

I shrugged. "I guess it's possible, I haven't caught a whole lot of TV since my trial. "

The bottom rack to my right spoke up. "You went to trial?" I nodded

"And you lost?" I acceded.

"Yeah, you did it."

"No, I really didn't."

Toilet Rack spoke up. "So, where have you been for the last week?"

I straightened up, "A one-man cell downstairs."

Bottom Right Rack said "They isolated you for a week in the hole? For what?"

I shook my head "No, not the hole, just a holding cell. I guess they just didn't have a bed."

Toilet Rack stood up. "Does it look like we are real tight on space in here?"

I looked around. "No, I guess not. Why else would they do that?"

"Bro, they're scared of you."

I shook my head. "No, that's ridiculous."

"Not really. What are you here for?"

"Well, three F-1's"

"Murder. Right? Do you know why I'm here? Misdemeanor probation violation."

"Oh, wow. That's crazy. Wait, why are misdemeanor offenders and, well, felons together?"

He threw up his hands. "Welcome to Miami County. No, there are two jails in Miami County. The old jail, here, and the IF. They usually send misdemeanor cases and real low cases to the IF from here real fast. Me and Patrick over there were kicked out of the IF for bad behavior so we get to hang out here with you higher felonies."

I realized that I still hadn't set my cup or spoon down anywhere. The empty top rack in line with mine had some belongings on it so I put my cup and spoon on the Pan style bed.

Toilet Rack introduced himself as Ron. Ron was five-five with sixty pounds on me. He wasn't fat or fit, rather, a healthy mix of the two. In the next hour I got to vicariously know some of the others in the pod. Beer Belly, below me, was Angus and the Top Rack in the far corner, a stringy intellectual with black hair was Mark. Mark and Angus were set to leave for "CRC" the next morning. CRC being the first stop for those going to prison, so I surmised. Patrick, the rack under my cup was caught "receiving stolen property". Dave, the bottom rack between Ron and Mark was in town fighting a case brought up while he was already in prison for manufacturing meth.

"Hey...uh Ron."

He stopped drawing a checkerboard on the top of his rack in pen and looked at me.

"What do we do all day, exactly?"

Patrick, an overweight thirty year old with cliché prison tattoos spoke up. "You're looking at it."

I looked around. "Do you ever leave here?"

He laughed, "If you are awake at six you can go to rec."

I nodded. "That's cool, where is it?"

He laughed. "In a room this size on the first floor, if you're really lucky you can go outside to the cage with a quarter basketball court and a flat ball."

I frowned. "Oh".

The click of the hallway door shook our plate metal walls and vibrated the bars. In walked two COs with a cart. Everyone in the block grabbed their cups and spoons and walked to the other side of the room. I followed suit and passed to the other side of the block for the first time. On the wall to my left was another toilet and a steel shower box. Drawn next to the box was a large, phallic like arrow and a sign reading "Jack Shack". The two walls that were barred had a wraparound table. Outside the cage on the catwalk was a TV stacked on top of white plastic tubs. In the bars was a slot four inches high and 18 inches long. My new roommates lined up and one by one received their tray and a cupful of Kool-Aid. I sat on the bench and ate the contents of the tray I had become accustomed to. They watched Jerry Springer, the five o'clock news and then a carefully negotiated series of shows.

I had been handed a towel and sheets from the CO and decided to visit the dubbed "Jack Shack." A soap, named all-purpose bodily sanitizer, was stationed next to the shower. I took off my issued flip flops and began to get into the shower.

Ron jumped up. "Whoa, whoa, whoa, what are you doing?"

I turned to see Ron. "Taking a shower?"

He motioned toward my feet. "Without shoes? No. Cleaned every day or not, six, now seven guys use that shower. Do you really want whatever we do in there on your feet? Put your shoes back on. Same thing to when you go to the joint. Sit on your shoes when you use the toilet, too. Trust me."

I put my shoes back on and stepped into the shower. The shower was a stainless steel rectangular prism with a shower curtain, button on the wall, black rubber mat, and soap dish. I slipped off my orange pants and shirt and put them and my towel on the towel bar attached to the wall outside the stall. I touched the button and a cone of high pressure water jetted forth from the nozzle about me. The high class body sanitizer smelled to the level of its name. It reminded me of an industrial hand soap used by a cheap factory. After a few minutes of standing in the spray I pressed the button to shut the spray off. After another thirty seconds I tried again and again. Finally I stuck my head out of the shower and asked Patrick how to turn it off.

"It's automatic."

I waited another five minutes in the increasingly hot spray. Eventually it shut off as abruptly as it came on. I dried off and walked back to my bed. At eleven the lights shut off and I fell asleep while they were still talking.

My studio apartment flooded with light in the mid-morning bliss. I stood up and walked to my stove. I put a half burnt pan back onto one of the burners on the stove with olive oil and walked back into the living area. My cat, Bodhi, wrestled with my blanket on the floor where I was sleeping. I watched him for a bit then moved toward the window. The traffic on the street was usual, and my landlady strode into the building in her usual brisk pace. I cracked the window to the sizzle of the oil and moved to my record player. Modest Mouse, Flaming Lips, I put Fleet Foxes on the table and spun the beginning. The song faded in as I cracked three eggs into the pan and turned down the heat. I turned on my heel and plugged in my coffee maker. In the cabinet under the coffee maker I found my girlfriend's cigarette roller who had recently given up smoking. I took it to my coffee table and took out a jar of tobacco. Opening the jar I uncovered a small metal container. I mixed 2 parts tobacco, one part cannabis in one cigarette and the opposite in another. I moved back to my food and shifted the eggs onto a plate with a bed of cheese. I poured three cups of coffee into a large mug and took the two back to my table. Before the record side had finished my breakfast was finished, the litter-box was cleaned, I was dressed, and I was out the door. I took the stairs to the first floor to check my mail and then the elevator to the parking garage where my bike lay. In the garage while the door was rising I lit the lessor of the two cigarettes. I smoked one in the morning with the 2:1 mix, one after school with a 1:2 mix and one in the evening with a 1:3 mix with a beer in those last weeks before my trial. In three weeks I had finals, lost my girlfriend to a bad breakup, mentally prepared myself for trial and had a murder trial. My parents never told me my final grades. No doubt I failed the majority. Even if I was excellent in school, which by no stretch of the imagination was I, I wouldn't have been capable of reasonable work under that stress. I biked ten minutes every morning, lightly puffing my illicit cancer, a rare reminder that I was still in control.

My eyes shot open with the lights turning on. It was time for breakfast. Not three eggs, coffee and a spliff. Just state food and beverage. In my first morning at the new block I noticed the black mold creeping from the corners. Long ago the blocks had been painted pink though the black cracked the paint and stained their attempts at dulling the pain of the place. A year later I can only look back and smile that I thought I would see my apartment in a matter of weeks. I would never see it again.

After a few days in my new block I began to find some type of routine. I would pull myself away from the poison of my thoughts through playing games like cards or chess, talking to the others in the block, watching the TV through our barred cage and working out. There was a phone in our block so I could call my parents as often as I wanted, so long as I had money on the phone account. Whenever I was bored I would shower or read or remake my bed again and again and again .. When two of the inmates left for CRC we changed our beds around so that now I was on the bottom rack near the only walled corner in the block. The beds looked like oversized baking pans with solid flat bottoms so once my parents sent me pictures I put toothpaste on the bottom and stuck them to the top of my little apartment in the jail. On the top rack, where nobody was sleeping, I put my books. Soon after going into general population we went to commissary. We made out orders at the beginning of the week by handing the CO an order sheet filled with our commissary selections. Then, toward the end of the week we would get ramen noodles, soap, shampoo, summer sausage, little Debbie's and anything else the jail could safely profit on. My clear tote with the minimal amount of commissary and several letters was tucked onto one side of the upper pan bed. This was life. I soon came to the understanding that I wouldn't be going home too soon. Then I would come into the understanding that I would be going home within days. I spent my days trying to stop myself from drifting back just a week, two weeks , three...when I had a life, I had friends. My family came and visited me just days into my stay in general population. "Visiting" consisted of thirty minutes separated by a glass panel with two other inmates on either side of me. I saw several of my family members waiting to talk to me. One by one they would cycle through and we would speak for a few minutes and then switch. The saddest speed dating ever. When it was over there was no notice. The phone shut off and we were standing in silence with the hard glass between. I was ushered out and soon found the block again. Early in the morning, before four in the afternoon that is, not many of the inhabitants were awake beyond our cage. I stood up on the bench, then on the table that wrapped around the cage and wove my arms through the bars. I could see them walking away, across the parking lot, across the street, to their respective cars and then off into the distance. My mind began to wonder across the street to the back of the strip mall where I could see the back door of my lawyer's office. I wondered if a new client was sitting in the plush chairs being told what I was told, being motivated how I was motivated that we were going to win, that the truth would prevail and I would be freed. I waited and watched the parking lot until I heard the toilet flush behind me. I turned to see Ron standing near his rack.

"How was your visit?"

"It was good, short, but good."

He walked around the bars separating the sides of the block and sat down at the table. "Do you want to watch the news? I think it should still be on."

"Yeah, that's fine." I said as I hopped down and sat next to him. He picked up a toothbrush holder and sticking his arm through the bars turned on the analog TV perched on plastic tubs. It sparked to life though instead of the news there was a comedy on one of the channels that we had both seen about a NASCAR driver. Watching the movie we laughed waking up the rest of the block and soon all of us were sitting near the TV watching and laughing.

"You look just like Ricky when he was running around the track screaming." I told Ron, laughing. Everyone laughed, remembering a rant Ron went on when he ran around the block after losing a game of cards. We all laughed at the movie and for just a moment I forgot about where we were, about what was in store for me and where I could be going.

I talked to my parents and they told me that they had been sending me letters along with many people from my church and around where I grew up. I hadn't received anything so I waited until one of the COs walked through and I asked them.

"Nope, nothing has come for you."

I asked if he was sure, if there was a reason my mail wouldn't get to me. He became agitated.

"Listen. You don't have any mail, alright?" He left and I was left wondering if what he said could be true.

"Hey, Solo." Ron called out from across the block. "Solo!"

I looked over. "Me?"

"Yeah, you. Haven't you seen that my boy? He named his son Han Solo, anyways, you're our son so you're Solo."

I laughed. "Alright."

"That guy was lying to you. They hold mail all the time. You should put in a complaint."

I took his advice and worded carefully a complaint that night which I turned in. Soon after, we were joined by a small kid with face tattoos, Abbott, and a larger guy who soon would be going to CRC, Flanigan. I sat with Flanigan and learned about CRC. I learned that I shouldn't associate with gays and child molesters (chomos) because nobody ever associated with them. People usually don't even try to steal from them because they are such outcasts. **Well not being noticed wouldn't be too bad.** He also told me that at CRC I would spend the first week in R-unit which is for reception and inprocessing. After that I would go to a formal block and before I knew it I would be at my "parent" institution. I took in everything I could, I tried to learn fast so that I could pick everything up before he left. While we were talking one day Abbott walked over and asked about a tattoo I had on my arm. I pulled up my sleeve to show a brightly colored array of nonsense.

"My brother and I drew it on Acid." I lied. I had learned from my first few days here that people would just get bored and walk away if I told them the truth that it's a weird tattoo because my brother and I are weird people. They however thought it was an awesome tattoo if I told them that we were stoned out of our minds on hallucinogens while we drew it. Unethical I suppose but hey, it's jail.

Peter

He came in with the short nervous steps that I quipped the attributes to a penguin with hemorrhoids. His hair was short and blonde. His face was unfamiliar except to Abbott who immediately sat up in his rack. I set down my book and leaned toward him.

"What's up?"

"I know him, he's a bitch."

James, just walking by sat down on his other side; "Who is he?"

"His name is Peter Janson. He fucked with my baby mama."

"That's Peter Janson?" said James. "He tried to hook up with mine too."

Ron's smile widened. "Want me to fuck with him?"

James and Abbott exchanged glances. "Definitely." said Abbott.

Peter walked into the cell and set his mat on one of the top racks. After putting his cup and spoon under the head of his mat he laid down facing away.

"Hey!" Ron yelled. Peter stayed facing away.

"Hey, Peter!" Still nothing as much as a twitch.

"Hey, fuck boy I'm talking to you." I sat up and put my feet on the floor.

Generally, the intelligence of this place, when accosted as such square their bodies up for a fight to determine masculine superiority. Instead he simply turned over and responded to the call.

"Yes?"

"So I hear you've been talking shit about my little brothers?"

He shifted uneasily but didn't answer.

"Are you ignoring me you fucking bitch?"

He rose to his feet and started moving toward Peter.

"I asked you a question."

Peter sat up and his eyes widened.

"You know what, get off your bunk. We're going to fight, bitch."

"No, please don't." He almost whispered the plea.

"What did you say to me?"

"Please don't hit me."

He grabbed the bars and started scooting toward the wall.

"Get the fuck down off that bunk."

"No... HELP!" He started slamming on the wall.

"CO! HELP! NoNoNoNO!"

Ron put his hands up and calmed him down. "We were just kidding man, chill out."

The lights kicked off and for a moment it was silent. Then Ron's voice broke through the darkness.

"Hey, Peter."

The silence persisted.

"I know you aren't ignoring me again."

"What?"

"You know hitting the wall this morning made you look kind of like a bitch."

Abbott and James chuckled from their bunks.

"Do you know that you're a bitch?"

An inmate was banging on the wall downstairs. No doubt he was drunk.

"Are you going to answer me or do I have to come over there and rip you off your fucking rack?"

"I didn't hear you."

"I said, are you a bitch?"

"...yes," he said it in a choked sob.

"Say it. Say I'm a bitch."

"...I'm... I'm a bitch."

Ron, Abbott and James broke out into uproarious laughter.

I stared up at the pictures of my family. All I could think about was how my life led me here. Me, a pacifist vegetarian who may not have made it to church every Sunday but who couldn't imagine treating another person like this. Ron's voice broke the silence again.

"Hey bitch, you know you really pissed me off today."

"How?"

"With all of that ignoring shit and because you got on the button. That tells me that not only are you a bitch but you are also a snitch which is much worse."

"Oh..."

"In fact, come over here and cuddle with my dude Abbott." James was still cackling.

On the other side of the room, "Didn't I just tell you not to do that ignore shit? Get over here and cuddle with my fucking dude."

He slowly came down off his rack.

"How do you want me to lay?"

Abbott, finally able to communicate between his breathless laughing, "Just sit here on my mat, we just want to talk for now."

He sat down and I breathed a sigh of relief. At least they were just making fun of him instead of something worse... And then all too fast it happened. Abbott, who was sitting across from Peter, jumped into the rack and started throwing punch after punch into him, then Ron who was sitting next to Abbott jumped up and started connecting punches into his side. James, who was sitting beside Peter, stood up and walking by me started stomping in a place where I would assume Peter's head to be. By this time I had stood and was moving into the day room with Craig who I'm sure was just happy to not have the attention on him. With the sounds of muffled cries low impacts and aggressive grunts Craig covered the camera while I stood on the bench to look out the window. I tried to put out of my mind what was happening. I looked outside and saw a woman walking down the street. I tried to imagine what her life was right now.

I bet she's a college student, I thought. *I bet she's going home to a loving family and needs to get up early the next morning.*

The cries crept through my defense mechanisms. Every time I got away from that room, away from that floor, that building, every time I got away from my life there; he would find me. His cries found me on the street with that woman. He found me at my parent's house, in Colorado, in Florida, every place I went to squeeze just a little serenity he was there. He found me. He finds me still through the darkness of my sleepless nights and every time my mind drifts back to that terrible place. It was the first time I really understood the second and third fundamentals: Nothing is free, meaning you must pay for everything you do. And, that disrespect is unforgivable. When I heard that it was over I retreated to my rack. He was still with me. He made me wonder whether or not it was wrong to just cast a blind eye. It also made me realize that this place worked under a fundamentally different set of ethical laws. On the outside I would try to stop such a fight because I didn't believe in solving misunderstandings through violence. Here, if you severed the predator from his prey you will be indistinctive from the prey. By standing up for Peter I would have greatly disrespected the other three and would have received the same treatment. Perhaps it would have been morally proper to do so if he was one of my own, setting these moral inequities to society aside for a moment I stared up into the pictures of my family. What would they think about such violence? Such barbarian justice? This was such a strange world.

"What do you think about what we just did?"

Their laughter sprung up into the night. Even Peter laughed slightly , unsure of what to do. I swung my legs over my rack and groped under my bed for the clear tote. When I found it I opened it and located a pen and some paper. I walked into the other hall of the pod where the light from the slotted holes in the walls lit up a small spot on the counter. An excellent spot to write, I thought.

"Feel like writing?" A voice came out of the darkness.

"Yeah" I said. "I can't sleep." I didn't mention why I couldn't sleep. I thought to myself and began a short story. It was a story of what had just happened. I sat up for two hours or so adumbrating the story that would become my fourth chapter of this book. I wrote across the top of the first yellow pen ridden page a single word. I named the story **Peter**.

Megaphone

I received a visit every week from my family while I was at county and the week before my sentencing my friends came to visit. Carl, Wendel and Laura were my best friends in the months creeping up on my trial. Wendel and I had known each other for eight years since we were both eight and in soccer together. Carl and I knew each other from school and we had begun hanging out a lot more since my criminal process started. Laura and I met in the spring just before my eighteenth birthday. months before my trial. She was 28, beautiful and she had a daughter. When we met it took little time before we started dating. Weeks before, just before my trial I had ended the relationship, fearing the worst and wanting nothing more than distance between the woman I loved and myself before I was sucked into the cyclone of fate. Wendel was the first one I talked to. He had the same smile he always had and we talked as if nothing was wrong, as if the glass and my jail-orange clothing were both gone and the two of us were just as close as we always had been. Carl was nervous to start talking to me, it seemed and once we began talking he seemed to be hesitant to open up to a receiver three feet away from me. I was sad to see him less than ecstatic, as he usually was, I entertained him with stories about what I had learned. I talk to him about Dave, the older man who had manufactured meth, I told him about Sickmann who was overweight and laughingly serious about his previous extensive prison experience, all two years. By the time he passed the phone to Laura he had his usual smile. Laura looked like she was just as sad to see me as I was to see her separated by glass. I wanted to see her smile and all I could think to tell her was a vulgarity. She smiled, though it was one knowingly of what I was trying to do. I wish I would've told her how I felt, I wanted to. I wanted to tell her that I wanted to want her to want me. I longed to tell her that I would have run away with her as soon as the trial was over, if I would have won. I ached to hold her and tell her I could still be with her forever. But I couldn't. The things I always wanted to tell her that were unsaid remained unsaid and the last thing I ever told her was a vulgarity. The phone cut off as we said goodbye, I watched them file out one by one, giving short nervous waves of farewell. When the last of them had left the sound returned to my ears as if it was lingering just far enough to give me privacy with my thoughts, the plaguing thoughts that I couldn't escape anymore. I was alone. My family were all with me, though it wasn't companionship. They stood with me out of a paternal love and although I loved them eternally I knew wholly that I wouldn't have a girlfriend again, or a wife, or kids, or a life. At least not for many years, not until I had escaped the pit I was falling into. It's depth I didn't know yet and in those days I still had an ignorant delusion that justice would prevail over the injustice of the courts, but soon I would know. The woman's voice found me. She sounded irritated, at edge and almost nervous. She demanded that I leave the visiting area. I stepped out of the cubicle that where I was waiting and walked through the crash gate to where she stood. She clutched her radio and nervously edged around me as I passed. I could have seized her radio, subdued her, then made my way to the stairway, down to the basement where it was rumored that you could make it to the court house. If the rumor was true then I would find myself in a building full of police officers. I would find an unsuspecting bystander in the bathroom, take all of their belongings and leave with their clothes and car to the highway, from there it was an open shot to the state line. I could have done it.

I could have ran. I thought as I laid down in my rack, hearing the cage close again. I laid in my rack wondering what would happen to me if I escaped. I would never be able to go to school, never be able to have a job, or a family, never be able to settle my case properly, never be able to see my family again. I could never escape. I could elude, but never escape. I could outwit, but never outrun. Eventually the inevitable reality would find me. I would realize that my existence wasn't life. That my life would only begin once I could relax, and every day that I waited and ran would be another day I would have to toil in the pit of despair when I finally decided to return. I looked up at the pictures of my family, the ones who had to suffer every day with me. I stood up and floated to the phone. I dialed for my parents and waited. I saw Dave sitting in front of the TV watching a NASCAR race. The others in the block were on the other side with the racks, playing cards and cursing NASCAR.

Within two rings my mom answered and put me on speaker. Everyone sounded so happy, a piercing sound in my mood. I tried to laugh, tried to sound as if nothing could possibly be wrong. Then it happened. For months my sister had been living with my parents and I got to spend an incredible amount of time with her and my wonderful two nieces. The hardest part of my entire incarceration would happen in three...two...one...

"Hey Patrick!" It was my niece, the older of the two who I had bonded with a great deal. I opened my mouth to talk and all that came out was choked breaths of air. The line went silent for a moment then my sister chimed in.

"Go play with your sister." I could hear her run off, I could hear my family understanding what happened to me, I could hear but I couldn't listen. The phone call was over before I knew it and time moved in an ethereal way. I floated through a lack of sensory input. I might as well have been alone in the block. I made my way to the shower and hit the button. I used the soap I bought on commissary and once I was cleaned I stood there, waiting for something to happen, anything. I was at the lowest I had ever been or ever have been since. I felt the high pressure water slice my skin, cauterize the wounds inflicted by the courts. I thought long to myself about what was happening. I closed my eyes and began talking to someone, anyone. I had attended church when I was on the street though never really prayed. I talked and talked and talked. I asked for help and support and just to be free. The water would turn off and I would press the button again and keep talking. I asked for my family to be okay and for my nieces to be safe and happy and healthy. I asked for help again, and again, and again. When the water turned off I reached for the button again but stopped. I felt a strong presence as if someone was watching me. I also felt like all of the worries had gone. Could it have been the hot shower? Or the praying? I didn't know, I just got out and dried off. I walked over near the TV and sat down. Just then Ron was walking in.

"Hey, Solo."

"Ricky, what's up?"

"Do you want to make a brick?"

Sure, I guess." We walked over to where the racks were and started getting the supplies together. There were three of us who were going to eat so we got:

- Six ramen noodle soups
- Two summer sausages
- A bottle of cheese
- Two pickles
- An empty clear tub

I took the soups and put them all in the tub. We turned on the shower and waited for it to get hot, then filled the bag with water. We waited for the water to cool then drained the tub and repeated the process until the noodles were cooked. Then we put in the ramen seasoning packets, summer sausage, pickles and cheese. We mixed the food and once it was done we measured equal shares for everyone and we ate. We made the new guy clean the dishes even though we only gave him less than half of what we got, and we laughed and joked until the lights had been turned off and we were sitting in the dark laughing and talking.

We turned the TV on once it got late and watched a show called Locked Up about the inside of prisons. We laughed when something relatable happened or when someone got what they deserved and I started to really feel a part of the society. Even with the memories of Peter, who had long since checked in and gone to a different block, I started to see the situation in a different light. If I didn't wrong someone, or a group of them , so egregiously, then I wouldn't be on the tail end of such a serious whooping. Although I still had distaste for violence in such quantity I understood and respected its primal purpose. One by one everyone left the TV until it was just Ron and I left alone. We watched a string of shows and talked through the night. I told him about my nieces and he told me about his daughters and his wife. He told me how he hurt himself at work and was put on painkillers, when he got addicted to the painkillers he started getting sick when he couldn't get them so he started doing heroin which was cheaper. After a while of doing heroine he needed money because he lost his job so he started robbing houses which led him to jail. He told me heartbreaking stories of a law abiding citizen being sucked into the pit and sympathized to a small extent to my plight. I told him that since he only had a few months left in jail he had to take advantage of the experience. He had to stand up and get back on his feet. He couldn't let this mistake define him because he may not get the chance to try again anymore. The night dragged into eternity and eventually we went to bed and for the first time even after such a hard day, I slept soundly.

When I woke up it was to the sound of my sister. I was confused at first, I followed the sounds to the other side of the room and listened closely. She sounded like she was shouting outside. I listened closely.

"We all love you! We all care about you! Don't worry, we will get you out!" I smiled. I love my sister so much, she was always very caring and sincere even when she had to go through hardship she would care for others before herself. I listened for ten minutes until she stopped. I sat down and turned on the TV, as was tradition of our mornings. On the channel was a protest on the news. I watched my sister with the megaphone yelling and lots of people I had met and hadn't met protesting the actions of the court. I looked wide eyed at the picture. I couldn't believe what I saw. When the story ended I sat back and thought to myself how incredible it was, How lucky I was to have so many people on my side. I smiled and thought I would be alright.

Oval Room

"The sentencing of Patrick McGail in the case 13CR437B."

I sat on my rack thinking that phrase over and over again in my head. The room was silent in the twilight hours of the morning. Sitting up I looked toward the windows through cage bars. I walked to the counter boarding the far side of the pod, I stepped up on the cold steel in my rubber sandals, and I gripped the bars and stared forward out across the parking lot toward my lawyer's office. I wondered if I would ever walk through the office again, shake hands with my lawyer, and sit on well picked business furniture to talk about my future. I wondered if he would ever make fun of my bow tie or if we would talk about the girls in our lives. I could hear the pod gate open but the officer's words were just a muffle. I gripped my glasses and statement tight and walked into the hallway. My shoulders ached, my knees were rubber. Was I walking toward the definition of my destiny? I kneeled on a bench and prayed for strength, for direction, for help. The shackles closed around my ankles and the cuffs around my wrists. Before the waist strap tightened around my waist I put my glasses and statement in my shirt pocket. The hallway before me narrowed. I had to go back to the room that plagued my nights, my days. The gate of the holding area before the court room closed behind me and I waited. With only a 4X4 box to stand the others that would come to wait and go on to court stood at the wall and only looked toward me in fleeting glances. I was unmoving, I was not empathetic to their comfort or how much space they had. If they had asked me to scoot over I wouldn't have heard them or headed their plight. I was stone, strengthened. The penal system was taking me; a shapeless form of clay, emotional and weak, and quickly carving the new me out of stone. I had been so stressed, so disturbed, so broken down that I had been built back up. I was being torn down from a foundation of sand and rebuilding on stone.

I stood up straight and walked into the courtroom. It was filled to the max with spectators, family members of both sides, media, lawyers and the judge. Taking my place next to my lawyer we sat. Him wearing an in fashion suit and comfortable smile. Me, orange suit and stoic expression.

{I must not show fear.}

The tension in the room rose gradually.

{I must not show pain.}

The judge read the charges and Ohio revised code entries.

{I must not show fear.}

The family read their statements.

{I must not show pain.}

My lawyer read his argument.

{I must not show fear}

I was asked to make a statement.

{I must not show pain.}

I took my glasses out and put them on.

{I must not show fear}

I unfolded my statement.

{I must not show pain.}

I took a deep breath.

{I must show no fear.}

{ I must show no pain}

{I shall be strong.}

{I shall endure.}

{Just one more step.}

{Just one more day.}

Apologizing for my inadequacies to prevent the atrocious crimes hot tears ran down my face. My strength faded, my fear was omnipresent. I took the glasses from my face and shoved the paper uneasily in my pocket. Blinded by the salted release I choked out final apologies. It was of no difference. They would never believe. I would always be, to them, the man that robbed and killed their son in cold blood. No appeals or retrials or amount of evidence would ever prove anything else to them. I sucked in a deep breath and sat down. My lawyer leaned in close and whispered something to me. I was oblivious. I was deafened. I was cold. While the judges dark black eyes peered down at me reading about my lack of remorse and finally my sentencing Latin and ambiguous state law poured over me. My eyes were dry once more and I was trying in vain to comprehend how much gravity this day would have on my life. I recalled meeting Antonio, my lawyer, for the first time. He had told me two very specific things. He would fight very hard for my freedom and that regardless of the outcome of the trial my life would be changed forever. I feared that at the time. I was a sack of Jell-O looking to meet a blacksmith's' forge. Even sitting at sentencing I had no idea what that really meant. Only now do I know what it means to be unequivocally changed.

When the sentencing was being read in spite of myself my mind wandered to Poe's *Pit and the Pendulum*. How I felt persecuted by the inquisition! My rights at trial had been stripped, my rights had been halted, everyone I knew had been led to believe the media that I was a kind of manacle, 21st century Charles Manson. The hooded man was reading my sentence. The verdict, twenty-four years to life in prison! Injustice was a fungus on the pizza labeled "no mushrooms!" This would be set right, but in how long? Would it take a year? Would it be my life's work to stop my life from being consumed? Would I just be in a ubiquitous cycle of following my fate to the new courts? Fresh injustice? Would I be severely stressed for such an extended time that I develop poliomyelitis, or a tumor? My immediate fate was sealed. I was going into the belly of their system. But I would get out. There was no way around it. Whether I was eighteen or fifty, I would get out. Whether it took a year or my life it would be set right. And if I left on my two feet, with a cane or in a box they couldn't keep me forever. I hoped. The pod was still quiet when I came back. I sat on my rack and stared across the room to the windows.

"What did they give you?" Ron's voice came from the cocoon.

"Twenty four years."

His head emerged. "Well, I mean it could've been worse."

I laid back on my rack, "to life."

He walked over to my rack. "I'm sorry, man."

I shrugged and rolled over. "It doesn't matter now... but thanks."

We sat in silence for a minute.

"What does 'to life' mean at the end of my sentence?"

He was staring off. "It's a life tell."

I sat up next to him. " I know, but what does that mean?"

"It means by discretion of the parole board you can be in prison anywhere between twenty four years and... Abbott, how long is a life tell?"

"888."

"Yeah, anywhere between twenty four and 888 years."

{I should get a hobby.}

I laid down and rolled over. Macqueen, Dufresne, Eastwood, Papillion, McGail. At any cost, at any length, I would be free. Through tunnels, across oceans, I would find a way. Appeals or barbed wire would be my key. I had to stay fit. I had to stay lean. I couldn't tell anyone. No accomplices, no witnesses, nobody. I would not allow my escape to be com—

"What are you doing?"

I looked at Ron, still sitting on my bed. "What? oh, just thinking." He stood up and started walking away.

"You know you couldn't get away." I jumped up and followed him.

"Don't act like you know what I was thinking." He sat down next to Abbott and looked over to me.

"Well, were you thinking about killing yourself?" I sat down adjacent to him.

"No."

He smiled. "Then you were thinking about running. You can't get away."

I shrugged. "Hopefully we won't have to find out."

The week went by in a blur. No longer was I interested in the simpletons coming and going. Tom, petty theft. Luke, assault. Bill, OVI. They would come and they would go. Almost always avoiding me completely or looking at me nervously. I was not blind to the news reports, nor was I deaf to the hushed whispers in the blackness of night.

"--what is he here for?..."

"--no... I don't believe you."

I cast a blind eye to all of it. The rumors, the looks, their games, their world. It was all a wash. When they would come back with a long face and ninety days on their lips. They would wail their discomfort and with a fleeting glance toward me of humor Ron would approach them and whisper to them. Without fail after looking at me with shame I would respond with derision and continue to read.

Thursday, the day before I was set to leave, Ron assured me that they would wait another week to ride me to the correctional reception center. However much I hoped he was right I packed all of my belongings into my commissary box and promised that I would wake them if I did leave. I lied.

No Good at Goodbyes

The wind was rushing past my visor and the cold spring air was seeping through the cracks of my helmet, biting my nose. The sun had long since set and I knew we must be getting close to the hotel because the smells of the lake were growing stronger with the freezing wind. I kept thinking if I didn't fall off my bike from exhaustion I would freeze to death. Over time I started to think I couldn't go farther I looked into the glow of my Dad's tail lights and was full of the same happiness that filled me when we used to go to ____

"Chow!" I woke up and felt the happiness leave me with the warmth under my blanket as I walked to get my tray. There were two new guys, I had neglected to ask their names or why they were there. Why should I get close to them when I'm leaving in just a couple hours? The hardboiled egg was cold and the milk was warm. *Typical* I thought as I choked down the last of the tray and walked back up to the slot to replace it. I went to my rack and laid down, hoping a sliver of my dream was intact for me, or at least that they could maybe forget me for another week so I can see them again.

"Hey, Solo!" I turned; expecting an explicit gesture, instead I saw Ron looking over at me with a serious almost sorrowful look. "Wake us up if you leave."

"Yeah, man" Abbott echoed.

"Okay, guys. I will."

I covered back up and slipped into sleep after staring at the words emblazoned on the wall for more than an hour, wondering when I would be abused mightily.

My brother was plucking an indistinct melody on his ukulele and I was admiring the lush valley below. I didn't know anything could be so beautiful a moment as this one. The cool rock arch beneath us was sitting twenty three or so stories high. The trek had taken all day but the view was well worth—-

"McGail, pack it up!" My heart sank. I had forgotten to call my parents before I left.

"Can I make a phone call really quick?" I whispered crossing the room so as to not wake everyone up.

"No, we don't let inmates do that. Just in case."

I supposed it made sense, they don't want people trying to escape. I looked at Abbott and Ron and decided not to wake them up. Walked to my bunk and quickly took apart and packed everything I had left out around my area. I put everything into the center of my mat and took it under my arm out of the pod. Derick closed the gate quietly, sensing I didn't want to wake up my friends. We walked out of the room. I wouldn't be in the room for a very long time, If I had known everything that would go on between my stays maybe I would have begged not to leave, or maybe I would have ran knowing everything good I would be running to. In any case, I was out now. Walking back down the hall all I could think about was how to stop this. How I could convince the staff that if would potentially behoove them to keep me for another week. The elevator doors closed and with the slight bump we began rolling downward. I knew that if they already had the documents for my release and transfer wrote up I had no chance. I would get on the bus to Shawshank, the train to Auschwitz, the boat to Alcatraz. It was the green mile now. No more pink bars and misdemeanor 2 offenders. I was going to the last true urban frontier, where men became gladiators and boys became women. Where everything was either a weapon or was edible. I was going to prison.

42

Staying Me

"Patrick!"

"What...what?"

"I said your name like four times ha-ha..."

"Oh, sorry," I said, slightly embarrassed that I didn't notice the doors open and more embarrassed because they were all waiting on me.

I shuffled out of the elevator and walked to the same bench I sat on for intake. My personal items were on the floor in a large hanging suit bag. I leaned down and put my small tote box filled with letters, toothpaste and books that my parents had brought me into the bag. Inside I could see the mail that the CO's assured me "never came." There was another guy sitting down there on the bench opposite me. I wondered whether he was an intake, just now starting his long journey or if he was leaving with me into the belly of the penal beast. He looked about my age; several inches taller perhaps with light colored short hair and a generous about of facial hair but younger than anyone I had seen in weeks. My suspicions were met when he was instructed to stand and approach the counter. They then had him sign all manner of forms from general release to property release to a money transfer that will go to CRC. I stopped paying attention to what they were talking with him about and reverted back into myself. I recollected everything I had been taught and ever heard about prison. Everything from my visit to Alcatraz when I was younger to the video game I played that taught me how to build one. I understood the basic logistics of how prisons worked, their weak points, and the psychology of people therein. I thought of Steve McQueen, Tim Robbins, Clint Eastwood, Johnny Depp; Every portrayal of what not to do and what to do in prison ran through my mind. In a society dependent on television my education on prison was plentiful. Whether or not any of it was in the least bit useful was yet to be seen.

After a quarter hour I was sent up to the counter. They were talking to me but the words were just white noise. I glanced only briefly at the papers I was signing: Release of property; curious, my mail isn't on there. Temporary release/transfer, I wonder how many of these are signed every day in Ohio. Release of money to the Correctional Reception Center. Please, I know I'm never going to see my money again I thought. I sat back on the bench and looked toward the holding cells. Fifty four days ago I sat in one of those cells and began this chapter, I wouldn't believe that this could happen. I never thought I would leave here without my parents on either side. I supposed the story can't end yet. There was a lot that still must be done, people waiting for me to meet them, places awaiting my presence. The CO's, being alerted of the chariot waiting my compadre and I, had us kneel on the bench where they put on the shackles we both knew oh so well. Hands and feet bound we walked through the steel gate out into the garage. To my dismay there was no school bus waiting for me; just a sheriff car.

The town of Troy felt so alien to me now. We passed first all of the places I had watched through my window for two months. Once we passed those we might as well have been in any other town in Ohio. The sentimentality I once felt for these streets and small shops had long since gone. In its place was a feeling of emptiness. I had no urge to deface the town nor attend one of its many festivals. It was the girlfriend who slept with my best friend after years of dating. I would never feel animosity toward this place, but it would never be home again. I didn't know then how right I was about that. I wish that I had slept more the night before. I was tired now and between the hilly country road after months of no movement and the football talk show on the radio I was quickly growing nauseous. There was no way I would sleep on the way, although my friend beside me was already snoring. *[Only an hour and a half left.]* The countryside stretched by and by. I thought it ironic that the sheriff was both speeding and rolling through stop signs. Small time country towns sped by. *[I wish I lived there]* I thought with each one. Eventually the sheriff pulled onto the highway. With the smooth straight ride I finally fell asleep. I woke up to the jolt of the car pulling off the highway and back into country roads. My amigo was awake and staring pensively out the window. In the distance I could see high steel wire fencing. *[This is it.]* We dragged closer and closer to the compound. I read the sign as we sped past "London Correctional Institute". *[Hi Dave!]* I looked to my left and saw a smaller compound. "Madison Correctional Institute". We continued on down the country roads. I wondered how much longer we would be driving. We entered a small town after some time named Orient. I knew we had to be getting close and sure enough when we got out the other side of the town I could see it in the distance. As it loomed closer I was reminded of the daunting presence of a prison I saw in a Wes Anderson movie once. We pulled behind the grounds following signs for inmate receiving. The Sheriff parked in front of a huge chain link gate next to a guard shack. I tapped my Kemosabe who had once again fallen into a deep sleep and we stepped out of the car. I felt the stiffness in my joints fall away as I walked past the cruiser.

"Stand over there in front of the gate."

We walked past the guard shack and stood at a section of fence between the two outer fences. On the fence closest to the compound there was a roll of razor wire on the top of the fence. Between the two fences there was ten yards of gravel. The fence closest to the outside had four rolls of 3 foot diameter razor wire stacked to the top with another on the top.

"This week is gonna suck" *[It speaks!]*

"Yeah it is, at least we are outside. I haven't been in months."

"Yeah, me either."

The wind was blowing across the compound and I could see small groups of blue dressed inmates walking around outside. In our orange we were standing out from everything. We stood there eventually shivering in our shoes for what felt like ten minutes.

"What are they doing in that shack?" I didn't want to know, probably nothing good. Just then I heard the crunch of gravel behind me.

"Listen." His voice was surprisingly high pitch for his large build. "Once you walk through this gate you belong to the state. Don't say shit unless one of these guys talks to you first. They will really give it to you if they feel they have to."

[Great!] I thought, the Sheriff gave us one final look and said something that has always stuck with me.

"Keep doing what you're doing and you will be just fine."

A large pair of state corrections officers walked us through the gate and to the large cement building marked "receiving".

Oh, Come on, I thought when my pulse began to rise. *How bad could this be?*

709871

[I wonder how many naked men this CO sees every day.]

I knew this would happen; standing completely naked in front of a CO whose job it was to check every orifice on my body visually to ensure that I'm not smuggling anything into the compound. It served a dual purpose though. By having us strip down first thing they showed us right away that they were in charge. From that point forward until I left the department of rehabilitation and corrections I would be told when to eat, what to eat, when to sleep , where to sleep, when to relieve myself and if they wanted me to strip down and spread my cheeks. I would have to do that too. To an extent I had done this at County but there I was hardly looked at. Here every mole, sack tattoo, birthmark and hair on my body was scrutinized. I was nothing. No, I was less than nothing, I was an inmate. Once he felt he had properly examined me I was allowed to don the state issue clothing. One pair of underwear, one undershirt, one pair of socks, one pair of plain blue pants and one plain blue shirt. From there I was told by the examiner to sit in the first room on my right.

I exited the examination room before my buddy and after turning right I took the first door on the right into a large holding cell. The cell was twenty feet by twenty with benches lining the walls and a steel sink and toilet by the door. I sat close to the door on the right side of the room and waited. A large sign on the wall read:

NO TALKING! WHEN YOUR NAME IS CALLED PROCEED TO THE FIRST WINDOW!

The hallway connecting this room had doors going into rooms just like this one on the right and a wall of tall cubicles on the left with windows extending down the length of the hallway. I started to look at the other people in the room and immediately remembered something I read on the internet: *Unless you are talking to someone never look at them; they will take it as you sizing them up and they may be compelled to fight.* I needed to learn how to assimilate fast so that I could just float by in this world outside of everyone's notice. I looked straight out the doorway at the first window and took quick glances using mostly my peripherals to "size up' what kind of people would be here with me. What I saw was exactly who I would have pictured here. There were a couple who looked like bikers, one had tattoos covering everything I could see of him and most of the people were black. I always thought Ron and Abbott were being racist when they said the population was predominately African American. But now I began to understand. I was the outlier. Slowly each of the people in the room were called into the hallway to the first window. What happened to them after that was beyond me but after the numbers began to lessen in the room I started to become less and less anxious until I was the only one left.

"McGail!"

I stepped out into the hallway and up to the first window. The woman behind the desk reminded me of the old secretary in *Monsters Inc.* In a way I thought it was ironic that this place was sort of in its own way a Monsters Incorporated. After telling her my date of birth, social security number and that this was my first "number" she stamped me on the right hand with the number:

709871

In a way, I thought this was mildly similar to how Auschwitz prisoners were numbered. Except their numbers would never wash off with soap and water.

"Go to the next window."

I walked to the next window and the man asked for my number. I felt that it would probably be a good idea to memorize it. After I signed a form indicating that I did not have any property the man pointed and instructed me to go through the last door in the hallway which was labeled "Quartermaster." All the same people I saw in the first room were in there plus another ten or so. The benches were completely filled and my friend who rode up with me was standing. I stood next to him and noticed that the room was exactly the same as the first except that there was a window on the side opposite me through which I could see what looked like a warehouse and next to the window there was a large trashcan. The walls in this room were also covered in dozens of signs saying everything from **"Don't talk!"** to **"All trash in the trash can."** Others told the reader to check the contents of the bag before we leave and to follow the red arrows once we were out. Slowly but surely each person went to the window, gave their sizes for shirts, underwear, pants and shoes. Received a mesh shower bag filled with clothes, put on a pair of black Velcro shoes and left the room. It felt like it had been an hour by the time I finally reached the window. I had no idea what size I was in anything but shoes so I repeated the sizes my friend had gave. When I put on the shoes I gave the inmate worker a copy of my intake property sheet and walked down the hallway following the red arrows. I came to a larger hallway with a small waiting area on one side with another large trashcan, doors that led to more holding cells, and more doors that led to anything from offices to a barber shop. Another inmate worker ushered me towards the waiting area where I found a clipboard that had a stack of half sheets of paper on it. I took a sheet and filled it out with the requested date of birth, name and number. I looked at my hand, but my number had already become illegible. Luckily, it was printed on my copy of the property sheet and I wrote it on the paper. *[7-0-9-8-7-1]* To my knowledge I was waiting here to go into the barber, as that is where everyone else was going. I indicated on my sheet also: my height, 6'2". My weight, 158. My hair color, brown. And my eye color, brown. When I was next in line for what I assumed was the barber a CO that appeared to have eaten a whole cow every day for ten years walked into the waiting area.

"Have any of you eaten?" We all shook our heads.

"Head to chow." I had to admit that this was a pleasant change, not yet had I had the freedom to walk anywhere for chow, Nevertheless walk myself to chow. The only problem was I didn't even know how to get out of the building. I elected to follow my friend who had the same experience as me though seemed to know where we were going.

"Do you know where to go?" *[I guess I was wrong.]*

"No, you?"

"No, but I think I saw some people walking this way."

Sure enough we found our way to an exterior door and once outside we followed a line of inmates to the chow hall. The chow hall had two lines going through it. One on the far left wall, and one on the right. The floor in between was filled with four seated tables that were in line with numbers on the front and rear walls. When a row was filled, say 5, the CO would call to go down the next empty row on that side. After a certain amount of time the CO would call for the row to leave. When I first entered the hall the first thing I noticed was Flanigan sitting at one of the tables closest to the line I was in.

"When did you get here?"

"Today."

"Try to get into A-3 when you get out of reception."

"Okay."

It was cool that I had a friend there. But did he say A-2 or A-3? *[Damn.]* I couldn't believe I already forgot. When I went to sit down at the seat my line led me to I noticed some people had on winter coats. Actually, everyone had on a coat.

"Hey man, where do you get the coats?"

My friend looked amused. "It comes in your clothes bag, dude."

I felt dumb. Maybe I just didn't notice because I had been in my head all day. I ate my meal of turkey, apple, water, potatoes and lettuce. The turkey was made in a kind of stew. Definitely better than anything I had eaten up to that point. I finished early and looked around. The population met the same general observations I had made up to that point. As I looked around

I watched them steal just about everything. Some put their plastic sporks in their pockets, others apples and one put his cup in his pocket. I suppose that we had all stole to get here, why stop now? We were called to file out and after finding one of the guys I recognized from the waiting area we started walking back to the admin building. I looked around for my friend and saw him walking toward a different building by himself.

"Hey!" He turned around.

"Wrong building!" He looked back at the building he was walking to then to the one we were standing by. He jogged back to us.

"All of them look alike."

It was true. In a way this place reminded me of a private school. All of the building were identical and we were in uniforms. We went back into the building and to the waiting area we were in before. The others in my group were ushered away and I was led into the barber's chair.

"One or two?"

"One."

"Are you sure?"

"Um, I meant two." It had been awhile since my hair had been that short. In two minutes my hair was gone. I thought I would have missed it more but I had bigger things to think about. Leaving the shop I followed the red arrows again to a room labeled "Identification." I went in and sat in a chair in front of an informally dressed CO. He asked me the questions from the site slip I gave him over again. Afterwards he took my picture and told me to go to the holding cell next door. I walked out of the office and straight into the cell. [*How many of these rooms are there?*] Everyone I saw at the quartermaster was sitting in there. I squeezed onto the bench and listened to the others small talk. This was a trick I used at County to learn how to speak without standing out. I learned that older convicts were referred to as "School" or "Old School". There was a distinct difference between inmates and convicts: Inmates were younger and wild while convicts were older and more laid back. Chomos were child molesters, the pod they stayed in was called candy land, and cell warriors were inmates that yell out the windows and doors until they are let out of their cell. While they were discussing the present economic state of various camps in the business of drugs and tobacco the nurse came into the doorway with a cart full of files. One by one she called us up and handed us large medical files and a green photo ID. I looked at my picture, I was so small I only took up a quarter of the frame. On the ID my weight, height, number and birthdate were printed along with the large word "INMATE." She led us through each page and had us number, sign and date each form. When we were finished we were all led into the room directly next to the door my friend and I previously left out for lunch. The ceilings were vaulted from 10 feet to thirty feet. At its highest there were skylights in the walls and large painted pencils on the opposite. The area closest to us had a large waiting area, a desk for the CO, three doors on the left going into offices and one on the right going to a physician's office. We sat in the chairs and one by one were weighed while waiting to go into the offices. I was weighed and went into the middle of the three offices where the nurse took my blood pressure, filed the file I had signed, and asked me a series of questions pertaining to my past medical history. After saying "No" around twenty times I left the office and approached the desk.

"Number?"

"7-0-9-8-7-1"

"Go to R-1"

"Yes, sir."

I left the building and directly in front of me was the dorm. It was the one my friend had tried to enter. I walked to the door and knocked three loud times.

The CO held up a finger and I rested against the wall. The day was beautiful, I was glad I was so lucky as to catch such good weather. The door clicked and swung open. He pointed to a large table in the middle of the pod to sit at. The pod was a large "V" with a desk at the point and cells lining each side of the branches that extended outward. On one side fifty chairs had been prepared in an assembly fashion and in front was the table at which I was sitting. An inmate sat at the other side of the table and walked me through another paper to sign. This one I didn't even try to read. I initialed down the page and signed the bottom. He handed me a roll of toilet paper with a bar of soap in the middle, a small yellow book, and instructed me to sit at one of the many chairs. I found a seat that allowed me to be reclusive without being obvious. I noticed that the inmate I had talked to at the table was not wearing his blue shirt, as were several others. I wondered what was special that they could stand out in such a way. Perhaps they held a staff position in the pod. A short plump CO walked in front of us after about half of the chairs had been filled.

"Shut up!" I hadn't heard anyone talking.
"Welcome to R-unit. I have one rule here, I don't care what you do in your cell; fight, fuck, or workout. Just do it quietly."

[*That makes me feel safe*] He then outlined the entire handbook we were given including the three pamphlets we received on House Bill 86/Senate Bill 337, an arbitrary orientation handout, and a leaflet with information regarding tuberculosis, hepatitis, staphylococcus aureus, sexually transmitted diseases, HIV/AIDS, and basic hand washing. All in all the ordeal took around an hour. Though I didn't listen to anything past the first twenty eight words. I was rather thinking about how long I would be here and what I would do when I left. When he was done he told us to lockdown. I looked down at my handbook and I saw the cell number: 2039A. I climbed the stairs and began reading the door numbers; 2005, 2006, 2007... There was a small group of one person showers... 2017, 2019, 2021... I followed the entire border of the pod and as I reached the end...2035, 2036, 2037, 2038... There it was. The very last door- 2039. I walked in and held my breath, there were two bunks. I would be locked in a room all day and night in the farthest part of the pod with some maniac.

"Everyone gets a roommate," I remembered the plump CO saying, but who would be mine? On top of the rack labeled "A" was a large black box, mat and pillow. Both sink and toilet were porcelain, and I had a window with bars on the inside that opened. I started to unpack my belongings into the box and heard the door shut. I turned, all day and all night I would be in here and seeing as everyone gets a roommate, I supposed this one was mine.

DC

He came in with a smile that reminded me of the Cheshire cat, as though there was nowhere he would rather be. As I started talking to him I noticed that his eagerness seemed to manifest perpetually. He was there for a parole violation. He changed his address but didn't think he had to tell his parole officer if he didn't leave the city. His hearing on the 22nd would determine exactly how long he would be staying but he was fairly confident that he would go home once he explained how he didn't understand the precise terms of his release. After unpacking and making my bed I laid down, entirely ready to catch back up on all of the sleep I had been missing. I closed my eyes and felt myself fall away into sleep—

"Hey, Patrick."

I was awake but pretended to still be asleep. He shook me,

"Patrick, man." I opened my eyes hoping that chow had already come.

"Hey, man. Are you any good at writing letters?" I wasn't sure I understood the question at first. After deciding that I had heard him right I shrugged my shoulders.

"Yeah, I suppose so."

His Cheshire smile returned. "Great!"

He pulled out paper and pen and started writing. I watched from my rack. I hadn't noticed at first because of how dark it was but he had tattoos all the way down both arms, and although he was easily 8 inches shorter than me he was much larger.

He spoke the letter he was writing and every now and then had me spell a word. For the next hour he wrote his brother telling him how there would be c-o-n-s-e-q-u-e-n-c-e-s if he didn't have his money when he got out and how he would f-i-n-d his a-s-s and b-r-e-a-k him down until he got it all.

Then he sent a letter to his girlfriend that said their r-e-l-a-t-i-o-n-s-h-i-p was over and that he would never talk to her a-g-a-i-n because she sent him to p-r-i-s-o-n.

It was interesting to meet a man my dad's age that had problems spelling not only complex words but f-i-n-d and g-i-r-l (which he almost fought me over because he swore it was spelled g-i-r-e-e-l).

I learned a lot about him from those letters. He read the Bible every day, he was getting social security checks, he had two kids and he was living in Dayton.

After he had finally finished he handed me an envelope and a few sheets of paper. I thanked him and got right to work on my own letter.

I addressed it to my dad.

Dad,

I was brought here to CRC yesterday. I'm sorry I didn't call yesterday. I didn't think I was being moved yet. Yesterday was boring. We got our clothes and were admitted to B dorm. I can say I already strongly dislike it here. Although, we go outside to/from meals (two of which are hot). I can't go anywhere without seeing someone I know; I saw a guy yesterday that I met in county. This is hard now; though I have faith, like you, that the end is near. Miami County may be corrupt but Ohio must see the problems that arose, right? Feel free to read any/all of the writings in my box that I released. For the book the only things I really need typed are the ones labled Skirmish writes? If you could, once I get to my parent institute

Could you send me the typed ̶s̶k̶i̶r̶m̶i̶s̶h̶e̶s̶ webs (after being photocopied) and a typed outline? The outline is the calender. To type it take the number on the penciled line as the heading and the events thereof as subheadings. Like this:

    1.

       • Verdict
       • Intake
       • And so on

Thank you so much for everything you and everyone has done so far. Never could I have made it this far without you guys and when the end finally comes I will know it's because we all made it together. I didn't think that I would be able to write you so

#2

except my room/cell mate gave me this
paper and an envelope. If you can, please
continue to push awareness in regard
to the _____ injustice. Not just
my story, but as many as possible.
It's not right that it just keeps happening.
I'm not positive, but from reading
the handbook it sounds like the visits
are real contact visits! Haha. When
I got here they cut off all of
my hair :(. I wanted to grow it out.
I'm going to start a mustache. I'm losing
my hair so I figure I should let other
hair grow. I guess that's what I get
for making fun of you for so long.
I'm trying to stay under the radar
as best as I can, which is

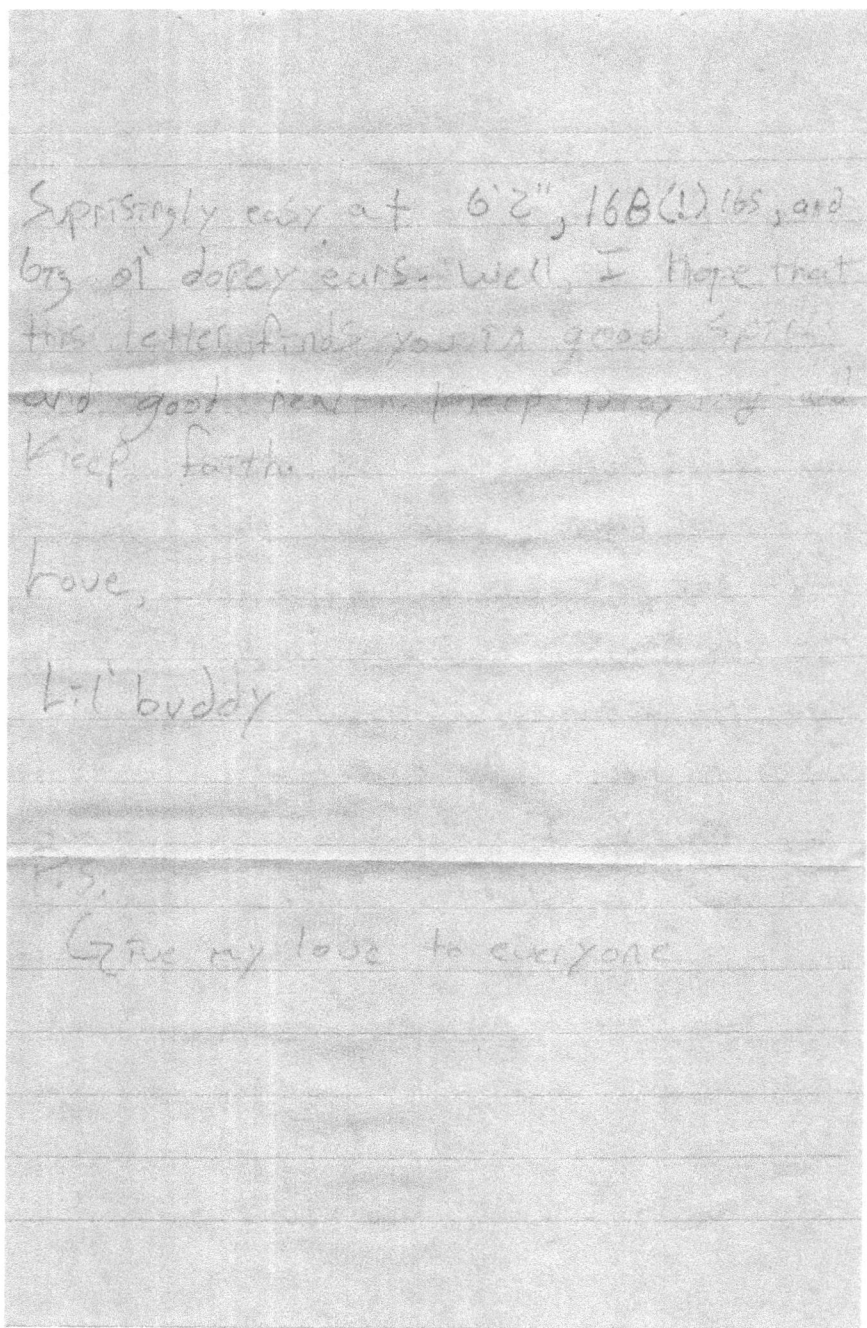

Sprisingly easy at 6'2", 16B (!) 165, and big ol' dopey ears. Well, I hope that this letter finds you in good spirits and good health. Keep praying and keep faith.

Love,

Li'l buddy

P.S.

Give my love to everyone

When I finished he noted that his handwriting was superior to mine. I agreed and praised him for his work. I then remembered Sickmann's note in County that people often compensated for the lacking quality of a letter's content with their handwriting. I smiled, amused that not everything Sickmann had told me was false. I laid down once again to fall into sleep. Once I was finally relaxed I heard a Titanic screech. It sounded like a meat cleaver met a chalkboard and held a rock concert. I jerked upward and saw that DC had pulled the heavy steel bed from the wall so he could make it. The screech was the sharp square legs dragging across the bare concrete floor. Shaking my head in minor disappointment I fell back into my bed, covered up with the winter coat I finally found and within an hour I was asleep.

"Hey, man. What's this word?" He had shaken me awake again.

I turned over and tried to focus on the page he was holding in front of my face. He was pointing at a verse in the Bible that read: "Now faith is the assurance of things hoped for, the conviction of things not seen." I squinted at the page.

"Which one?"

He frowned and pointed at the word while holding the book closer to my face.

"Um... assurance."

His smile returned again.

"As-surance assurance!"

I couldn't help but smile. For a fifty-year-old man with homicidal tendencies and a near elementary mental aptitude he had a certain charm and one thing was certain, whether he understood the word or not he was trying and definitely wanted to be closer to God. I laid back and stared at the ceiling. Though I had prayed in County and had been raised Catholic I wasn't sure I had faith. Whenever I tried to believe, as hard as I tried it always fell away. Perhaps I could learn something from this man who was sounding out words in a book with a reading difficulty comparable to Nietzsche's *Thus Spoke Zarathustra*. He sat back. He noticed me looking at his Bible.

"Do you want to read?"

Before I could answer he had put it in my hands. I didn't know where to start. I read stories when I was in school but didn't ever go much farther. I opened to a random page and started reading. Jesus was praying in the garden the night before he was crucified. I remembered reading the story but continued all the same.

While Jesus was being nailed to the cross I heard the CO at his desk yell, "Get ready for chow." I gave him the book back and put my coat and ID on. I stood by the door thinking about what I had read. I always took the Bible as a helpful philosophical guide to life, not absolute truth like most proclaimed and believed religion was just a clever way to extort the fearful so as to control the masses with a strong yoke. But now I indulged; if thousands, no millions of people over the last 2 millennia believe with all their hearts that Jesus was sent as the only true begotten son by God himself to die on the cross so that our sins might be forgiven, maybe there was some truth to it. The door clicked and I walked onto the catwalk above the range below. But then again everyone in the world for thousands of years believed the world was flat and that the sun rotated around the earth. But if we weren't made by something, then what? Was this all just a random mistake? The creation story from *Bulfinch's Mythology* corroborated the Biblical story, could the Greeks have just taken the Old Testament as truth and based their polytheistic religion off of it? We were wrapping our lines around the door. Ancient records from around the world spoke of the Great Flood, the Shroud of Turin was known by many as the cloth Jesus was wrapped in before being laid in his tomb. And I did feel something while I prayed at County. We were walking outside now: lining up on either side of the road; top range on left, bottom rage on the right. I didn't know. And I still had so many questions: If all of this was real, then what? What do I do? How do I "Come to Christ?" How do I create a real, lasting relationship with Jesus so that I could go to heaven? Had I denied him for too long? Was my old self destructive/promiscuous ways too much for forgiveness. I needed to ask someone, but who? I had enough trouble speaking up against what I knew was wrong. How could I ask someone for these things? Surely my bunkie didn't have the answers, did the Bible? While I was walking in my line back from chow I asked silently if there really was one omnipresent, omnipotent, all powerful God could he give me guidance? I know I would need someone with real drive in my life to help me learn just how to come to Christ.

All that night I kept hearing the story of how my roommate's brother and his brother's wife insisted that he trust that they will keep his money and stuff safe. Every time he told the story he would end it by saying that he just had to keep faith and trust his brother. Then after forty five seconds or so of silence he would sit straight up and with more fury and mannerisms than I had ever seen and he would describe in grave detail beating, humiliating and killing his brother and wife. After this, I fell asleep more scared than I had been in weeks.

[*Oh, come on. How bad could this be?*]

I woke up several times throughout the night to my bunkie shifting in his sleep, flushing the toilet, yawning/yelling and when the lights first turned on he got up and made his bed. I stayed quietly awake trying not to spark up conversation. Dozing, I waited for chow to come again. After around an hour we went out and walked to chow in the same lines as before. The air was cold, really cold. I was thankful I could finally go outside but also that I had remembered my coat. Grits, butter, two bags of milk, and two boiled eggs. I could have gotten coffee if I had wanted it, but I would rather sleep the day away. Looking around I saw several people stealing their milk and I thought I had seen one person go through the line twice. [*I must just be tired*] The walk back took less time than the walk up. I hardly noticed walking in the dorm until I was already laying down and without any trouble I was asleep again.

We were riding, we must have been close to Kings Island because my leg felt the fresh tattoo and it was warmer than up near Cleveland. We twisted and turned up and down the winding hills. The air was warm but after 5 days I was ready to rest. I couldn't believe how free I felt. This was the best time I'd had in a—

It was already chow again. DC had been reading the Bible and left it open on his bed, I walked past it and read an underlined verse:

"Pay attention to yourselves! If your brother sins, rebuke him, and if he repents forgive him, and if he wins against you seven times in a day, and turns to you seven times, saying, "I repent", you must forgive him."

I thought about those words on the way to chow. I hoped that they had reached my bunkie with clarity and insight into his situation. I decided I would ask him later in code. At least if he learned to forgive his brother then I didn't have to hear about his possible future crimes. Remembering at lunch how hungry I had been the night before I put my apple in my pocket to save for later. I justified it. They gave it to me so it's not stealing and I could eat it wherever and whenever I wished. I heard from the table to my right DC telling the story of his brother. By this point I knew it down to the dialogue

"Trust me DC man. If I get out man and he's…"

Maybe reading about the brother sinning just jogged his memory. I wished I could persuade him that violence wasn't the answer. Or maybe if I tried I would be as bad off as his brother. I held my breath walking out of the chow hall knowing there were CO's who spent all day everyday looking for people taking items out. When I succeeded I counted myself lucky. Back in our dorm later that night I brought up the forgiveness of one's brother.

That just fueled his story more. Now he would speak both parts of dialogue between him and his brother as he beat him down. When I brought up that he should forgive his brother again he started yelling passionately

"But what should I do? I'm not living with him. I'm not living with my Mom. Nah, nah, nah."

I shifted the conversation in a silent moment and asked what the prisons he had visited where like. These stories were almost worse. He recounted how his friends would rape various people down to the muffled cries for help and his yelling "shut up and take it."

I was interested in a way why he was so exuberant about these stories. Maybe it was because he watched horror movies exclusively as a kid, or it would have been that his father killed someone with an axe when he was a child. Both were certainly plausible and I wouldn't have been surprised to hear a crazier series of events. After every story I could imagine that would give me nightmares he finally went to sleep. Just as I suspected I fell asleep and awoke several times throughout the night with vivid dreams of being robbed, beaten, tortured and killed. At breakfast I drank two cups of coffee but to no avail as I fell asleep right after breakfast.

The next two days I went through the same routine:

- Woke up at 5:30 to DC making his bed,
- Go to breakfast
- Fall back asleep
- Go to lunch

- Come back
- Read through my handbook and pamphlets
- Avoid talking until dinner
- Go to dinner
- Come back and talk to DC about his brother, girlfriend and prison until one or two (judging by lights out at 11:30 and subsequent CO checks)
- Stay up for another hour waiting to clear my mind of everything he said and to make sure he was actually asleep.

Monday was the same, I had hoped to get out and start going through the process of reception, but it was Columbus Day and I would have to wait until Tuesday. That meant another night of carefully dodging every subject imaginable to set him off. However, he did teach me a great deal about who not to associate with in prison, what not to do and where not to go.

For that, I was thankful.

The Angel and the Messenger

Tuesday came faster than I could have imagined and with it came an early morning. Once the lights kicked on we were out of our cells and sitting in the assembly of seats. At first I thought we had already gone to breakfast and I had just forgot until I looked at the clock; five forty. When I looked around everyone seemed to still be asleep. Actually they all looked fairly harmless. As though they didn't get scary until after their morning's coffee.

A girl came in pushing a cart that read "BIOhazard" on the side. She was 5'5", slim, brunette, early 20s and extraordinarily beautiful. When she walked in from outside, the pod went silent. Every head in the assembly watched her cross the room. Her flowing hair was tied loosely in a ponytail that reached between her shoulder blades. Every step she took was ethereal yet echoed deep into the heart of every man wearing blue and white. She was an angel in Dante's prison, here to show us the heaven that lay past those gates. Her hand reached out for the doorknob to the room where we would be giving blood and as if in slow motion looked over her shoulder to the on lookers beyond. Completely unashamed we doted on the most beautiful creature we had ever seen. She was perfect. And then, she was gone. Hidden behind glaring panes. As soon as the door shut the room went wild. The words on everyone's lips were that of our fair maiden. Some said she was beautiful, others openly stated how they would... Well, you know. One by one we were walked into the room. While I was in line chow was called and everyone from the pod besides us six in line filed outside. From where I was I could feel the cool morning breeze and smelled the rain in the air.

"Next!"

I walked into the cool room filled with an on-the-go blood bank and went to the first empty chair. It was hers! I opened my mouth to speak but she was the one to fill our void with words.

"Roll up your sleeve." [*Make a joke*]

"Make a fist with your hand" [***Come one, what's something charming to say?***]

"Let go the fist, nice vain" [***Want to see another?***]

"You can go now."

I left and was ushered outside by the guard into the rain. It was pouring and I couldn't believe that I hadn't even said one word. What was really surprising was how was she completely dry? ***[Because she's perfect, duh.]***

I walked by myself to the chow hall, taking my time to take in the rain. I had always been one to enjoy rain, it was my opinion one of the most beautiful kinds of weather. The line for chow was almost nonexistent and by the time I walked up the length of the room I didn't even have to stop to grab my tray. I walked to the first open table and sat down. Cereal, cake, eggs and milk. ***[Huh, familiar.]***

I only had time to eat half before my row was called and I had to leave back out into the rain. With my coat I really couldn't complain, though. And the rain, unlike the air, was quite warm and made me feel perfectly comfortable. The row I had gotten up with was not in my dorm so when they started going down a different road I split off and headed toward my own. Surprisingly I wasn't accosted by a CO about where I was going and I walked right back in. I sat in one of the chairs that were set up and waited for further instruction. One of the inmates in the white shirts (I found out that they were porters and they did work around the pod) noticed me and walked over. He asked why I was here and who I was, I told him my name and a little of my story and he was taken aback. I felt an impulse to tell him about my recent light reading of the Bible and asked if he had one. He retreated into his cell and came back with a little brown Bible, he also said that he would pray for me. I didn't know what to say so I thanked him and put the Bible in my shirt pocket. He shook my hand and went back to his work. I wondered if I could ever be devout to a religion like that, there was so much peace and I longed to be devoted to something, especially if it could get me out of this place. Most all of the new people from both pods were back, all in all around 50. A woman had walked to the front of the room and began to address the audience. She was from the rehabilitation side of the organization and gave us information on drug programs and various early release programs at parent institutions. I wasn't eligible for any early release programs and for the most part didn't listen to any of her speech. When she passed out a survey screening who would be eligible for drug programs I scored as a 1/10 when it came to whether or not I had a drug/alcohol problem so I figured I wouldn't be attending any meetings any time soon. What I couldn't get out of my mind was the generosity and eagerness of the Christian porter who had given me the Bible. Maybe this was something I should really give a serious effort while I was incarcerated. I didn't know after all at that time how long I would be locked up so when is a better chance to try to find God than during these hardships? There were other talks after hers on the education programs on site and at other parent institutions. When all of the talks were over it was half past ten. We were locked down and I sat down with the intention to see what the Bible was really about. I figured what better place to start than the beginning? I opened to the first page:

"The gospel according to Matthew: Chapter 1: The book of genealogy of Jesus Christ, the son of David, the son of Abraham."

In an hour and half before we were called to chow I had nearly finished Matthew though I had more questions than when I started. My roommate had talked to me all the way out of the dorm and to chow and most of the time I had been reading but I hadn't heard more than 10 words of what he said. For the most part he had been talking and responding to himself, which seemed to suit him fine because as I discovered over the weekend, his was the only word that mattered to him and if allowed he would openly talk to himself.

My knowledge in reference to the Bible was quickly being refreshed from what I learned in school and now all I needed was to see someone with true faith that activity prayed to God to remind me just how to do it. I needed a nudge in the right direction and then someone's example to work off of. Coming back from chow I was excited to finish the book of Matthew and then see the apostles and Jesus in action again for round two: Mark. I finished the last few chapters of Matthew and realized my roommate never came back from chow. I closed the door figuring he just saw the nurse or someone and opened back up to the next book. Though, as I read I realized this book was the same as the first with some of the words changed. I remembered that the first four books are the same story told by different points of view. They were called the four gospels. I decided that by reading I would just learn them more clearly and kept reading. When I was at a good stopping point I put the Bible down and laid down. It was nice to have the cell to myself for the brief time DC would be with the nurse so I closed my eyes to sleep. No sooner than I had gone to sleep I heard a loud knock on the door. I looked up and saw DC staring at me with a wider smile than I had seen yet.

"I found you!" The door clicked and he strode in.

"What do you mean found me?"

He put his ID in the window and walked back to his rack.

"You didn't go to R-2 for the second lecture, they told us to go there right after lunch." *[I should **probably start listening** to those]*

"Did they say anything important?"

He was full of energy drinking from the sink, making his bed, looking out the windows.

"Yeah, lots of really important stuff, man. You should have been there."

I didn't think I would have gotten a whole lot out of it but bit the hook anyways.

"What kind of stuff?"

He looked out the window and frowned. "I don't remember exactly, but the minister and some lawyer talked to us."

I shrugged. "Oh well, I'll pick that stuff up along the way."

He fell back onto his bed. "Yeah, where were you anyways?"

I recounted the story to him, how I came back and read the rest for Matthew, some of Mark and took a nap. He just laughed and started a letter to his Mom. I noticed then that he started every letter exactly the same.

"I hope that this letter finds you in the best of health and spirits."

It was probably something he had learned a long time ago and used every letter ever since. I thought about going to God formally in prayer, and I realized that not only did I not thank God for what I ate, I didn't thank him really for anything. So while I was spelling for him: H-e-l-l-o, S-p-i-r-i-t-s, h-e-a-r-i-n-g, c-r-e-a-m, c-h-o-c-o-l-a-t-e, G-o-t d-a-m-n (even though I was sure the expression was God damn) and a-i-n-t; I thought and planned how to start talking to God. First, I would start my regiment of prayers again and add the "Our Father" to it. And then I would start thanking God for everything I could think of. The rest of that night brought chow, and more of DC detailing plans against his brother. Ready for the day he doesn't have five hundred and fifty three dollars exactly when he first sees him. When he finally went to sleep I remember turning over towards the wall and starting my daily repentance-

"Forgive me Lord, for I have sinned. In choosing to sin, and failing to do good I have sinned against you and your church. I firmly intend to make up for my sins and to love as I should, Amen."

After repeating it 10 times, saying 10 Hail Mary's, an Our Father and the Profession of Faith, I cleared my mind and without a single dream or fear, I slept. I woke up in a peaceful state of mind. DC didn't wake me up when he made the bed and I slept all of the way until they called for morning chow. I felt like a weight had been lifted. Not all of it, yet. But a fair amount of stress was just gone. Oatmeal, bread, jelly and bacon. I was nervous to eat the oatmeal after what DC had said people did to it. But after I saw him eating it ferociously I decided that no babies were wasted in it so I ate as well. When we got back to the block while we were walking back to our room the porter caught me;

"The lord spoke to me last night, you should read one Corinthians: Chapter 10, Verse 13."

Once again I was speechless. The first night I really reached out was this a sign? I got into my room and opened up right to it.

"No temptation has overtaken you that is uncommon to man. God is faithful, and he will not let you be tempted beyond your ability, but with the temptation he will also provide the way of escape, that you may be able to endure it."

Could this be referring to me leaving God and losing my faith? Or that my situation has an escape and through him I may find it? I didn't know what to think. But I knew that I was going to pray again later that night.

Anger and Answers

Sure enough I began to seek refuge in my free time with reading the Bible. It seemed like every time I read I found something to help me through my day. The unwavering devotion of the Apostles was astounding. When they were imprisoned and beat in Acts 5:41 they rejoiced that they could be counted worthy to suffer dishonor for the name of God, and after Christ's death they continued to spread the word until all of them, besides John who was exiled, was executed in the name of their savior.

I couldn't argue that their faith was true. Even when I had my doubts, thinking that this religion was no different than the Greek myths I came across the second letter of Peter that read "For we did not follow cleverly devised myths when we made known to you the power and coming of our Lord Jesus Christ, but were made eyewitnesses of his majesty." 2 Peter 1:16.

It seemed that every time I had a doubt or a question God provided the answer. I had turned myself wholeheartedly to Christ and my life was already getting better. I spent nights with DC, once the lights went out, watching the fences beyond my window while he was telling his stories. I noticed that there were roaming guards that checked for breaches. In addition, white cars circled the compound 24 hours a day. Flood lights were placed at regular intervals and seemed to turn on with the roaming guard's movement. I was not per se planning to leave. I just figured that there was no harm in observing my environment thoroughly. Wednesday brought fingerprinting, filling out visitation sheets and speaking to an administration officer that asked if I had any prior numbers and preferred camps and whether or not there were inmates I had problems with. I told her that, if possible, I would like to stay at CRC as a general population worker because of the low violence level and excellent facilities and as a precaution gave my co-defendants names for separation. If I came in contact with them I didn't know how I would react. If I would be mad for them lying or forgive them for their indiscretions as Jesus had taught me. I prayed for the latter; however, in the moment I suppose anything could happen. I was finding myself praying while I was walking around the camp and increased my night's prayers. I had only prayed once on my knees, when DC was out of the room, because I felt that praying in front of him went against what Jesus said in Matthew

"But when you pray, go into your room and shut the door and pray to the alter who is in secret. And your father who sees in secret will reward you." Matthew 6:6.

I felt like I would be praying in front of him just so that he could see me which would lead to vanity, then to pride which as I remembered was a mortal sin. That night I fell asleep during DC's stories and when I woke up in the morning felt as if my fear had been taken away. The burdens of my sufferings were getting taken up more and more every day. And sure enough I remembered something I had read in Matthew. I opened my Bible up and it read

"Come to me, all who labor and are heavy laden, and I will give you rest. Take my yoke upon you, and learn from me, for I am gentle and lowly in heart, and you will find rest for your souls. For my yoke is easy, and my burden is light."

I had begun the footwork of repentance and turning my life over to God and sure enough when I was weary and when I needed answers I was finding them abundantly in God. Sure, I wasn't speaking in tongues or witnessing awe inspiring miracles but I mean, come on, it was just the third day. In the morning after breakfast we were assembled and quickly ran through the dentist and psychologist. The dentist took a full x-ray of my mouth, measured my gums, documented my fillings and noted I had enlarged lymph nodes and a buildup of plaque on my tongue The psychologist also gave a basic examination to make sure I wasn't going to kill myself and that I had a fairly decent support structure. When he was satisfied he released me to lock back down.

I happily did so and slept the majority of what was left of the day. I couldn't help but be excited that I would finally be leaving B-unit. DC shared my excitement and further hoped that we would be bunked together again so we could throw commissary food "together" to make bricks. I remembered the warnings I received at County from people that would try to take advantage of me because I have money on my account. I decided to test him and his generosity.

"I don't think I'm going to have money on my books."

He looked devastated. "Why??"

I told him that rarely would I ask my parents for money. He insisted that I would have to get money so that "We" could eat good. I silently prayed that I wouldn't be bunked with him again. He continued all night that he wouldn't be bunked with someone that didn't get money. That he needed to "eat good" and if he had someone that didn't have anything he would either extort them or tell them to leave. Just before the lights kicked off he changed the conversation.

"Do you know anything about law?"

I had to admit that though I wasn't ready to take my Bar I had fairly adept understanding of everyday law concepts. He was nervous that he wasn't going to be released at his hearing and asked me to read the paper his PO had him sign to see if it said anything that would give him a hint of its outcome. I read the paper and right away my heart dropped. The paper waived his rights for a hearing.

"What does that mean!"

I wasn't entirely sure but I had a feeling he wasn't going home in a week.

"Which lines did you initial at the bottom?"

There were three options; admit, admit with mitigation and deny. When he pointed to the admit columns my heart sank further.

"DC, why are there two charges? I thought you just had an address charge."

He looked befuddled and tried desperately to read the paper.

"That says you changed your address and caused harm or attempted to cause harm to your girlfriend."

I understood right away why he said his g-i-r-l friend sent him to p-r-i-s-o-n.

"Well, how much time do you think I'll get? 45 days?"

I scanned the paper.

"This says that the APA recommends 180 days out of the 571 possible."

His smile vanished. "Well, at the hearing I can argue-"

"There isn't going to be a hearing, man...your PO had you waive your rights to the hearing and admit fully to both charges."

He stood up and crossed over to the window.

"What does that mean?"

I was heartbroken even more so because when he was talking about chopping his brother to pieces I prayed he wouldn't be released.

"It means you are guilty and you accept the punishment."

"But I'm not guilty?"

I could have cried. "You signed a paper that says otherwise."

He laid down and didn't speak until after the lights had kicked off. When he spoke again his anger wasn't toward his brother, but his PO. Now I understood why felons couldn't buy guns legally. We talked all through the night and stopped only when he fell asleep. I prayed that he would be filled with God's strength and that he could be given the virtue of peace to make it through his hard times and not do anything to return to that terrible place. When I was finished I fell asleep hoping that he would turn his life around and give his life over to God.

My legs were soaked from the waist down. My friends and I were walking back to my house from a small swamp we had been hiking in. Outside my house I came to my small stash of fresh clothes. I peeled the wet pants off and replaced them with a dry pair. Walking into my house I saw my mom, her face red with anger.---I was driving now. The only true way to make me angry was to hurt my sister and he had done it. I was extremely protective of my family and if he was still there---

I woke up in a cold sweat. I forgot how mad I was that night. Luckily, he hadn't physically hurt her and was gone long before I got there. I would never be driven to kill him, but what *would* I have done if he was still there? I was just happy I had the serenity and growing peace that had been rekindled and strengthened by Christ. I couldn't go back to sleep but I stayed awake and thought about my family. I didn't have the pictures above my bed anymore which was probably why I hadn't been as stressed recently. The lights flipped on and DC didn't move a muscle. I got up, flushed the toilet and made my bed as close to an exact impersonation of him as I could. He shot up in bed.

"What are *you* doing? You woke me up, you need to quiet down."

I smiled and with one last screech lay down. With a few hours until chow and then the excitement of moving pods. I closed my eyes and fell back into a deep sleep.

Chow came and for the first time I saw the lines of inmates getting ready to go to their parent institutions; Pickaway, North Central, Lancaster. A hundred inmates shivering in the cold of their fear and dread of mass strip searches. When we got back from chow they started reading the list of those of us who were reassigned. One by one for four hours we watched everyone leave who came the same day as us. One by one we steadily got angrier. Every time the phone rang we would run to the door then would hear

"...2037B... Pack it up!"

Then we would walk back to our racks and lay back down. Then we would hear the phone again and we would run straight to the window

"...1022A... Pack it up!"

We walked back to our racks and laid down. When the phone rang right after 11:20 count I didn't even get up.

They said, "2039!"

I jumped up and started packing. The CO climbed the stairs to our range and walked closer and closer to our cell. Our door swung open and we both paused to hear the moment of truth.

"Roosevelt, pack it up!"

We looked at each other.

"...should I?"

He shook his head. "No, sorry. Maybe Monday."

I beaned the clothes from my hand into the box. DC couldn't have been happier. He was beaming as he packed the rest of his belongings He shook my hand quickly and left. I swore loudly and was fuming. *Monday? Monday?!*

I couldn't spend another day in this cell let alone a weekend. I don't know what I would do. *Monday?*

My Dad's letter that I got the day before said they would try to come up to visit me on Monday. Not now because of the way visitation was set up I would have to wait until the following Monday when my last number, 1, had visits. *Monday?*

I could have broken a window, flipped a bed, I could have...then like a small switch flipped I stopped. "Be watchful, stand firm in the faith, act like men, be strong. Let all that you do be done in love." (Corinthians 16:13-14)

Rather than collapse at this small upset I should stand strong, knowing that God's will doesn't always follow our time frame. I shouldn't have cursed the world for not delivering me, I should have rejoiced that my friend was delivered. After all, I did pray the night before that I wouldn't be bunked with him. I calmed down, put my mat and box on the other side of the room and laid down. Before I went to sleep I repented for my haste to such anger, asked for strength and if his will be done, if he could deliver me from here so that I could see my family on Monday. I peacefully went to sleep. My door clicked open thirty minutes later.

"McGail, pack it up!"

B-1 1014

I couldn't believe my ears. "Where am I going?"

He smiled. "B-1, 1014B." I jumped with excitement and started packing. "You have ten minutes to pack up."

I threw everything in my mesh laundry bag and was out the door nearly at the CO's heels. I stopped, remembering my soap. I went back into the room and threw the bar in my shirt pocket. My yellow handbook lay on my black box. I grabbed it and walked back out. Half way down the catwalk I passed a porter with two cleaning buckets who was waiting to clean out my cell. When I reached the stairs I heard his voice.

"You forgot your I.D."

I hurried back and grabbed it with a smile and quick "thank you." Walking back to the stairs I heard his voice again.

"Do you want your towel?" I couldn't believe I had forgotten so much. I hurried down the stairs and waited below for him to drop it to me. With all of my belongings in one arm I caught it with the other. While stowing it in my mesh bag he reappeared over the railing with my cup filled with hygiene. I forgot everything. I set my possessions on the ground and caught the cup with only my razor falling out and hitting the ground. I tossed the cup in my bag and walked to the table where my week had started. I handed my pillow and handbook to the porter and walked out the building. The weather was immaculate. I praised God on my walk for such an incredible day and thanked him for the patience and love in which he answered my prayer. I walked down the curved streets with my mesh bag thrown over my shoulder. I didn't have a care in the world. I read the dorms as I walked to get oriented. R-2, A-1, A-3, A-4, I had to cross to the other side of the camp to reach it; B-1.

It looked the same as all the others. Hopefully it wasn't as monotonous and I would have such a bunkie from my prayers. I stopped in the space between the outer and inner doors and knocked. The CO looked at me from his desk then back down to his work. I remembered him from a day he worked in "R" unit.

He was a USMC veteran that had long lost his love of physical fitness and replaced it with a love of Cola and Little Debbie's. He sported a goatee and I suspected he was having marital problems due to the latent repressed homosexual tendencies and the fact that he brought his problems into work with him. I caught myself judging his shortcomings and remembered Matthew.

"Why do you see the speck that is in your brother's eye, but do not notice the log that is in your own eye..." Matthew 7:3

I submitted to the words and saw two inmates walking down the path toward me. They entered the small waiting area outside the pod and asked where I had come from. I told them and they seemed to not be surprised.

"For real, this POD is only slightly better than R-unit. R-Unit is a shit sandwich and B-1 is just shitty."

I couldn't help but laugh, and here I thought I was walking to the Hilton. A key turned in the door behind me and it swung open.

"You guys going to the hole?"

The two behind me laughed, one sported a white visitation badge.

"No, we got it all worked out."

He smirked revealing yellowed teeth. And the cold smell of grizzly wintergreen.

"Are you sure?"

They looked at each other and then back at him. "...sir?"

He crossed his arms on top of his round body and pointed his nose in the air looking down on them.

"Which one of you flooded your cell?"

They answered together, "flooded our cell?"

The bigger one with the badge spoke up again. "We didn't flood our cell."

His smile vanished. "I'm sure, let me find another pair of cuffs. Stay here."

He walked into the door next to us that led to the other pod and several offices including the sergeant's office. We were silent and I shifted uneasily from one foot to the other. I looked around at the cells. They were all empty. The large CO returned and flared at them.

"Go upstairs and clean that mess up."

Without even noticing me he walked back to his desk. I figured it best to remain aloof and walk to my cell. I walked the boundary of the left wing and read the doors. 1007, 1008, 1009, 1010, 1011, 1012, 1013, 1014. I stood by the door and finally noticing me the CO spoke up.

"Who are you?"

"McGail, I was told to report to B-1, 1014B"

While crossing the room I spoke. He cocked his head to one side once I was done, his eyes widened and his lips pursed.

"Excuse me."

I actually stopped completely taken off guard that he was so offended by my words.

"McGail, I-"

"Do you want to go to the hole?"

I was fairly certain I couldn't go to the hole for anything I had just done.

"No, I-"

"Why are you here?"

His condescending tone mixed with his rising temper was putting me at unease.

"I'm from R-1, I-"

He cut in, clearly not willing to allow me to complete a thought.

"And you just thought you could walk anywhere you want?"

Now I was starting to get angry. "No, I was assigned to this POD."

He was confident he had won.

"Ah-ha! But how do you know what cell, you just thought you could choose anyone you wanted!?"

He was yelling now and I wondered just how often he was such a nimrod.

"I'm assigned to 1014B."

His face flushed with anger. "I... you...sit down!"

I sat at one of the silver tables and waited patiently. Looking around I saw them dispersed around the pod. They were the same kind of tables from the dining hall. On the right wing there were bunks on the floor in the space between the three walls. The CO came over.

"What's your name?" It was a wonder he remembered who **HE** was.

"McGail. Patrick McGail."

He frowned. "I don't have any record of your transfer. You say you came from -"

"B-1"

"And you're going to..."

"B-1, 1014B"

I didn't intend to be so short with him but I was nearing the end of my fuse.

"Wait in the TV room."

I stepped in and the door closed behind me. Sitting down at the table I smiled.

At least I'm not bored.

After a half hour a porter came in with a paper on basic hand washing, a cloth piece with "1014A" printed on it, a name tag for the door of my cell that read, "McGail, White, 709871, 10/17, 1014, A" (I supposed that they had told me the wrong bed), a bar of soap and a roll of toilet paper.

"Listen, they will have a CO come and give you an orientation once everyone else arrives but I'll just tell you a couple things first. First, this is the worst pod on the camp, period."

This sure wasn't what I had expected.

"Why is it the worst?"

He nodded his head toward the CO desk.

"Our CO's are the most strict. They will actually look for arguments so they can have a reason to put us on Cell Isolation (Cellise) or take us to the hole. They're petty for real. The rest the CO doing the orientation will tell you or you will pick up. If you have any questions, ask. I need to get back to my work."

The TV room was silent once he left. The room was no bigger than a standard living room. On one side of the room were a stack of chairs on the other side was a blue screen with a keyboard attached. I remember reading about these computers. They were called JPay. On it I could send emails, ask questions, check my basic information like camp, funds and visits, and once in general population I could do video chats with family and friends. I wanted to register so I could get started but I didn't want to get in trouble again on my first day. I saw it was 2:15 on the screen of a small television set in the corner of the room. With all of the chairs I imagined that the TV room filled to the windows when it was time for rec. Slowly other people from "R"-unit came in and sat down in one of the seven chairs. When they were all filled a baby-faced CO came in timidly and stood in front of us. He spoke quieter than any other CO and called us "guys."

It was then clear to me why after ten or twelve years the COs turned into what we saw. When a lot of them first came they probably thought they would be like Adrien Brody in *Detachment* and help us by treating us like human beings. When they realized most of us weren't human beings they started treating us like the scared, angry, fit sacks of meat we were. What this CO stumbling through an orientation probably didn't realize yet was that some of the people he talked to worked very hard to get here, some people I met did things he couldn't even imagine in his worst nightmares to get here, and out of the latter many had nothing to lose. There was a reason why his utility belt was equipped with a man down button, why ambulances went in and out of most prisons daily, why some had to have their own hospitals. He didn't work in a correctional institute, he worked in the jungle.

I watched the inmates from my new pod coming in from outside rec. I watched for someone to stop at the corner cell, 1014. They filed past the door one by one. I watched every face expecting each and every one to stop at the cell. When none of them did I shifted focus back to the CO giving our orientation. He was making a joke about how hard it would be to break out of the prison. He was probably right. Short of a freak natural disaster just about nothing could break us out of here. I started to try to silently pray for strength and safety. Before I could finish he told us to go stand by the desk. I walked out and gathered next to the others. Next to me was a kid I met at R-unit. He was 19 and had 20 years to life. While he and his brother were robbing their grandfather his brother shot his grandfather three times in the head while he was still in his wheelchair, killing him.

I couldn't say much. My charges weren't much better and my sentence was longer. At least he could be with his brother in prison. I envied that. As I expected I was told to go to 1014A. I walked to the door and with a click I opened it. Walking in I saw that the right side rack was occupied by a guy laying down reading a book called *The Unseen Essential.*

I walked to the rack on the left and started unpacking. On my rack were several papers. One was a calendar through May. Another looked like either a workout schedule or score sheet. I threw it and a stack of checker pieces away. I wondered what kind of papers I would leave when I left. Once my box was under my rack I made my bed, I laid down with my new testament. My new roommate was still hidden behind his book and I figured I would take the opportunity to read some myself. I opened to the book of Romans, chapter five. "Therefore, since we have been justified by faith, we have peace with God through our lord Jesus Christ. Through him we also have obtained access by faith into this grace in which we stand, and we rejoice in hope of the glory of God. Not only that, but we rejoice in our sufferings, knowing that suffering produces endurance..." I heard the rustling of paper and in the corner of my eye I saw an outstretched hand.

"Hey man, Kerry."

Matthew 10:19,20

Once again God's loving grace delivered.

Not only was my new roommate a devout Christian; but he had a near unparalleled knowledge of the Bible, had also found God through tough times, wasn't sociopathic and gave me a cup of coffee! Apparently, he had been praying to God for the courage to break the ice about God and when I sat down to read the Bible he had taken it as a sign. He was interested in becoming a minister when he was released and loved talking about God. While he told me about what he had learned in regards to Jesus, forgiveness and the Holy Spirit I marveled at the energy and enthusiasm in which he talked about God. He was a natural born salesman. Charismatic, enthusiastic, knowledgeable, friendly and, most of all, he knew how to appeal to his customer.

"I used to sell crack, now I sell God," he would say.

As he talked he would stand up, sit down, use his hands, make jokes. I hadn't known what true faith was until I met him.

"God's got this," was one of his favorite sayings.

Every time he was stressed or over encumbered he would take a breath and just say "God's got this."

It was refreshing. He was also writing a manifesto of everything he was learning through the Bible. He called it "Jesus Teaches." It gave the basic student of the Bible knowledge on everything from how and where to read the Bible, how and when to repent, what heaven meant to him and how to get to it. It was clear almost immediately that when he decided through and through to abstain from drugs he had taken up and became addicted to God's word. When he rested just after four thirty count I sat back, taking in everything he had said. I looked over at him, once again he was engrossed in his book. I couldn't see his face, but a tattoo on his neck became exposed reading "Lil Scrappy." He had a picture on the wall of four kids and one exposed from his Bible of a woman. Two Bibles rested on his box, a small brown one like mine and a larger one containing both New and Old Testaments.

I shifted my gaze when I felt he had noticed me staring and looked around the room. It was the same setup as my last room, except that the window was half the width and double the height of my previous one. Besides the layout the room also had a schedule of laundry days and recreation periods on the wall next to my bed. There were more drawings on the walls in this one, mostly religious in nature. One read "Gospel Gangster." Another, "God bless this tank."

I assumed my new roommate was to blame for it. The CO's voice rang through the pod.

"Get ready for chow!"

My bunkie hopped up, pulled his blue shirt and coat out of his pillowcase rendering it flat *[how odd]* and slid past me to the door to grab his ID. He was several inches shorter than me, thin yet with the telltale signs of a growing belly that could soon lead to adult onset obesity. He was clearly ten years my senior and had well defined laugh lines. I stood up and he handed me my ID.

"Do we get pillows?"

He laughed, "Well, we're supposed to. I just put my shirt and coat in the case like you saw."

The door clicked and we walked out of our cells and off to chow. In prison one thing that is ubiquitous is routine. Everything revolves around it. It is necessary if you are to survive for any extended period of time. Ron called it "Bit mode." Once you got into it days seemed to fly by. For me all it took was those first two weeks in "R" unit and then B-1 to find it. At times it felt like a dream, one moment I would be in my cell, then the chow hall. I feared once or twice I had narcolepsy. I would be sitting in the nurse's office or the chow hall and briefly forgot how I got there. The key to bit mode was to block out the outside. When you thought about outside, how long you had to stay there, how your family was or anything outside of yourself and your new life you would make the days feel like weeks. But, once you realized that you were just a cog in some great machinery any amount of time was possible. A month, six months, a year, ten years, twenty-four years. It didn't matter. Every day was the same and after a while they all felt like they ran together.

The chow hall was surprisingly quiet, after I finished my meal I looked up at the line. I saw my neighbor in line with a different pod. I looked at the table behind me and sure enough his seat was empty. I knew I had been seeing the same people getting back in line. I wondered how they did it.

"Eight, take it out!"

The row next to mine stood up. With it one person from my row stood up, too. He walked out with the line and when I looked outside I saw him walk right up to the back of the line. *But this food isn't even good...*

When I walked out of the chow hall I followed the crowd, I walked into the line on the left side of the street and waited, I didn't see my roommate anywhere. Suddenly I heard his voice behind me.

"Hey, bunkie!"

I turned around and he was waving for me to go over to him. When the lines started moving I crossed to the other line and fell back to where he was.

"What's up?"

He shushed me and I saw the CO looking my way. He whispered from the corner of his mouth.

"You can't be out of order, definitely not in a different line. They will flip out."

I thanked him and looked over to the COs who had just come on duty. One was tall, wore a five o'clock shadow, sunglasses and arms the size of my head. The other was a short older woman with short white hair and a permanent scowl. The duo, as I learned, was named Spitler and Hitler. I wasn't sure just how bad they were but I didn't want to find out. We made our way back to the block. The cell had cooled considerably with the window open while we were gone.

"Why are you called Lil Scrappy?"

He smiled and spoke while stuffing his pillow. "Because I like to scrap."

I could see the appeal. Some people, *a lot* of people throw away just about everything. I had considered once which was more wasteful, to throw things away because you didn't need them or to buy things you didn't need. I brought up an interesting verse I had read earlier to him.

"Therefore, if anyone is in Christ, he is a new creation. The old has passed away; behold the new has come." I found that faith came quickly, like a wave. I was overjoyed all the time with an incredible peace. I wanted to tell everyone about what I had found. I attended church four times the week between services and bible studies, my only friend was an aspiring pastor and I only read Christian books. I was overwhelmed with faith. Though as soon as I would leave CRC my faith would retreat and I would lose sight of what I was trying to find through it. I would replace my god with other things until many months later.

We talked about how true that was. Late into the night we discussed everything we could think of. Mostly God and the word but also my last bunkie, how he had caught his last two, his case and when, at last, he inquired of my story I told him the same story I had told for nearly a year. When I finished we talked about the easily corruptible nature of the judicial system. How conviction is all they have ended up caring about. He asked why even with the thought of so long in prison I could remain so chipper. I told him that it was easy. I knew that if I got my appeal in six months everything would be okay. And, if not, I would still be okay. Regardless of what they thought they took from me I knew that God would take care of me through everything. He was impressed by my faith. Besides my family, my faith was all I had. Without faith I would wither like a dead flower. With it they couldn't take anything from me. I still had my family, I still had my God and I knew every day I woke up that I was one day closer to getting out, finding a nice beach and telling my story so that hopefully this could never happen to anyone again. Although I knew it was naive I wanted to change the world.

Sure enough I woke up on Saturday morning and smiled, one more day down. By lunch I had read my Bible for the day and was sitting idly on my rack. Kerry handed me a book, *Silenced*. It was part of the series Abbott had been reading at County. Kerry had finished reading it and was wondering if I would like to read it. I obliged and opened to the first chapter. It was a fictional Christian book about the rapture. I was almost immediately engrossed. The author was a literary genius when it came to keeping the reader in suspense. Before I knew it the CO's voice once again rang through the pod.

"Get ready for rec!"

I sat up and started getting my shoes on. The paper on the wall read "Inside rec, 2:30-4:10" for Saturdays.

"Sorry I won't be able to go out with you, I'm on cell restriction. My advice to you for today is just sit back and watch. You'll see how everything works."

He had me down to a 'T'.

"Why can't you go?"

He nodded his head toward the window. "I got put on cell restriction for ten days for yelling out the window."

I did just as he said. First I took a shower in one of the eight available showers. **Surprisingly, there was no wait.** Then I went into the TV room and watched how everything operated. First, the table in the corner of the rec room was only for those playing dominoes, one of the tables out on the pod floor was reserved for playing spades, the rest were filled with various cliques of friends. Aside from the gang tattoos and under the rug bartering it reminded me a lot of high school. Just as I had expected chairs filled the entire TV room. And just about everyone was filled. I sat two chairs away from a three hundred pound "baby mama", **not to this day do I know why he was called that,** and one chair from a large man with "Blood" tattoos. I did this to show to any onlookers that I was unfavorable to gay inmates, as was custom, and was accepting yet unaffiliated to any gangs. I watched the TV trying not to make eye contact with anyone. It was a football game between the Raiders and either the Browns or the Bengals. I couldn't read who and I didn't watch football enough to know by sight. I primarily watched so that I could blend in. I cheered when they cheered, I booed when they booed and I clapped when they clapped. Listening in on conversations around me I learned that there were two major currencies exchanged; "lopes" and "shots". I hadn't the faintest idea what either a lope or a shot was but from what I could tell they were both something used a lot and people wanted them both badly. From my left I heard a deep voiced man say

"I got my l'il dude gettin' me some weed so I'll be able to get that to you in a couple few days."

Surely they didn't have drugs here, that would be preposterous. Later, back in the cell I asked Kerry.

"Yeah, they have pretty much everything here, or at least at your parent institution. Drugs, cigarettes, tattoos, girls..."

I remembered DC talking about girls enough and didn't need to hear about it.

"...how much does stuff like that go for?"

He put his book mark in his Bible and set it down.

"It all depends on what you want. A deodorant cap of tobacco leaf is twenty dollars, cigarettes are five dollars, a pouch of tobacco is fifty dollars, a light costs fifty dollars, a teaspoon of pot costs between fifty and a hundred dollars, if you bring some to a parent institute you can sell a bottle of baby oil for twenty dollars. If you already made it into tattoo ink you can sell it for a hundred. A bag of BBQ Grippo chips at a parent institution can go for twenty dollars, Neurontin pills are a dollar fifty for 300 milligrams, a Suboxone strip costs a hundred dollars, heroin goes for fifty dollars a balloon, does that answer your question?"

My mouth was agape.

"Yeah man,. some people pay their bills from prison. It's not too bad."

I had to fight to speak. "How...do you know all that?"

He chuckled, "well beside this being my fourth number I had a store at my last number."

I asked him to elaborate.

"Well, I stocked up on food and acquired some foods, like Grippos, that you couldn't get anywhere else and sell them at three for two rates."

"What does that mean?"

He set his feet on the ground and recounted how and why the "store system" worked. He would give "Joe Schmo" two soups today and then on store day he would get three soups back. This was really popular with people that frequently gambled. They would go broke, take a loan out from a store man and buy back in. Another popular business was when chow hall workers would fill trash bags up with popular foods, hide the bags under trash in trash cans and then after one of their friends takes the bag back to their dorm they would sell the food out to people who wanted more or never went to chow to begin with. I was amazed. In the course of several hours he told me how each prison's economy generally functioned, fluctuation of prices between camps, and how drugs and tobacco were "keistered" in.

This would be the most interesting year at college I would ever have.

Just before I fell asleep I broke the darkened silence. "Kerry, what are lopes and shots?"

A Hug Long Overdue

"I don't know, man," he said as I put my coat into my pillow. "I'm telling you he could really help."

I sat down on my bed and grabbed my book. "...but I already have a lawyer."

He turned from the toilet and flushed. "You have one, yes. But if you get the public defender's help you could have a whole building of them in Columbus working on your case."

I thought of Antonio's firm and the law clerks that had worked tirelessly on my case.

"That's true. But..."

"Think about it. Here's a kite. At least talk to him."

I guess it couldn't hurt to talk to **someone** about what was required to get an appeal and if I fit the requirements.

"Here's a couple, actually. You can kite religious services, too. You could use chapel and bible study."

Apprehensive, I took the request forms and began writing:

A709871, McGail, 10/20, B-1, 1014, CRC, Public defender, other. I would like to speak to a public defender in regard to my jury trial. When he came in to ask for names that last day at trial I was not present and even though I have an attorney at this time handling my case I feel like it would be a good idea to get an unbiased, third party opinion to talk about the process and requirements for appeals, what to expect, etc... My case number is 13CR437B..

I glanced over at Kerry's kite he was filling out. I mimicked his ending.

"-God bless".

I folded the kite according to the folding lines and set it in the manila envelope plastered to the wall with deodorant labeled "outgoing mail and kites." I sat back down and started the next kite:

A709871, McGail, 10/20, B-1, 1014, CRC, Religious services. I would like to attend Christian Bible study and church services, God bless.

I folded this one as I did the first and stuck it in the makeshift mailbox.

Well, you can't say I didn't try.

I thought back to my desire to be moved to general population on the camp rather than at a separate parent institute.

A709871, McGail, 10/20, B-1, 1014, CRC, case manager, case manager. I would like to discuss my pending request to be assigned to cadre' at CRC. God bless

Now I'm in business.

I sat down working to recall what my handbook said about kites.

"You can expect to receive a response to your submitted request in around five business days."

The day was cloudless again I noticed as I was walking to chow. They had been since the day I surrendered to Christ. I felt like God was smiling upon me for finally returning to him after so long. Every day I had stepped outside I silently thanked God for such beautiful weather. I heard the sound of fists connecting with meat when I entered the chow hall. Half of the hall was standing and watching a far corner. The only thing that could be heard over the CO's shouting to "Get back in your fucking seats!"

I heard the impacts of the older thick white man's skull connecting with the younger one's face. THWAP! The CO's were wading through the crowd of onlookers to get to them. THWAP! More uniformed guards were running in from across the courtyard THWAP! The younger's face was covered in his own blood. THWAP! He was limp and fell to the ground. Ugh! The elder's grunt could be heard over all the talking and yelling as he was tackled to the floor his head connecting with a steel lunch table on his way down. Thud. The fight was over. Within seconds after the escort of both men out of the hall everyone was seated and the lines were moving regularly again.

"Hey, fee-fee-rick!" Kerry's voice boomed from behind me.

I looked over the cafeteria counter to a worker on the other side. He smiled and they made small talk briefly while we were walking past.

"What's a fee-fee?" I asked, sitting down at our seats.

"Well...," he started, speaking like a parent giving the birds and the bees talk.

"...When an inmate has been down a while, he rolls two socks over his arm, puts a glove over it, turns it inside out, fills it with microwaved lotion and ..."

"I got it, thanks."

Suddenly I wasn't in the mood for grits. I ate my scrambled eggs and bread and waited for our row to be called out. Meanwhile, a kitchen worker was mopping up where the two inmates had earned a one way ticket to the hole. While we were walking outside we emptied our trays in the trash can, put our cups in a crate and threw our spoons in another crate in front of a CO who makes sure we don't steal them.

"What's the hole like?"

Kerry turned around with a smile on his face from my last questions. "I can't tell you for sure, I've never been there. All I know is that it is in the basement of that building there."

He nodded toward a building near the main gate.

"It's also the only place on the compound without cameras."

I sped up to get next to him. "Why aren't there any cameras?"

He seemed to be wearing out by my endless questions and quieted when we caught up with our line near a CO.

"Well, back around 1990 there weren't any cameras really. They were added after a large number of complaints were being reported on abuse from the guards."

I remembered hearing about it at County but brushed it off, thinking they weren't serious.

"They beat inmates up?"

"Nearly to death, if you stepped out of line at the wrong time they would lay you out, get in a fight and you would come back from the hole with a broken arm and a wired jaw."

I shivered, perhaps due to the breeze.

"So there still aren't cameras in the hole because..."

"Because that's the only place they left to the CO's, yes. It's not too bad, though. Just don't go to the hole and you won't have to worry about it.

Back in the cell I stood facing the wall urinating.

Father, Son and Holy Spirit I bless this tank. Let no weapon made against it prosper.

"Did you write this?"

He was deep in his book and waited for me flush to answer.

"No, I never write on the walls here, they say if you do you'll come back."

Funny, I never took him to be superstitious.

I sat back on my rack and read more of my book. I very much enjoyed this Christian book, it gave me insight into the real sense of brotherhood that devout Christians felt. It was something I envied. It was something I wanted. That night I had dreams that I was being dragged down into the earth by one of the CO's. They threw me into a cell with moist cobblestone walls and, after beating me, left me in the dark. Waking to the CO calling for chow I was reminded again of Edgar Allen Poe's *The Pit and the Pendulum*.

I just hoped a revolutionary would save me before I fell any further into the penal system. I had nearly forgotten what my dad had said in his letter until I was back in my cell after chow. I had a visit! I didn't know what to do with myself. It was the first time in two weeks I would have talked to my parents and the first time in three months I could hug them. I was so nervous walking to the visit that I could feel my heart pounding in my throat. To get to the visitation building I walked past a steel door that read "segregation" and walked further toward the main entrance for the COs and visitors. I walked through the door that read "inmate visits" and stood with four others in a small alcove before the examination room.

A door next to the door read "Stop! Knock and wait!" Periodically the guard called for another person. As each of the inmates walked into the room more came in from outside. I walked into the room after waiting ten or so minutes.

"Place your ID and visit pass on the desk."

The room had a holding bar on two of the walls. He had me place my clothing on one of the bars and visually inspected me to ensure that I didn't have anything besides my appendages and my clothing. When he had decided there were no knives or nuclear weapons on or about my person he handed my ID and pass back and allowed me to pass by him and continue to the visit room. Before the room was another waiting area with a hallway and bathroom branching off of it. There was a desk for the CO to sit at next to the door reading "Visitation".

The visitation room had a small vending area near the inmate door, an elevated desk for the CO's to watch all visits, a children's room with books and toys and approximately fifty sets of chairs and tables. Some had one chair on each side of the knee high table. Others had as many as five chairs on one side to the one opposing chair. My parents were both standing at the desk for check in and smiled at me sadly. Before I had crossed the room they were both walking into the sea of chairs and tables to sit. I approached the towering desk on the far wall and handed the CO my ID.

"Name and lock?"

I was confused when he said "lock" but soon came to my senses.

"McGail, 1014."

He looked uninterested and handed me back my ID.

"Have you been here before?"

I was scanning the tables to see where they had sat. "No."

He pushed a paper filled with rules toward me. I glanced at it and noticed it was the same rules I had read in the rule book. I looked at it blinking for a second then handed it back. He gestured behind me and when I turned around I saw my parents sitting at the table just ten feet from me. I couldn't believe it. I crossed to them and embraced first my Mom then my Dad and we sat. Over the next four hours I recounted everything that had happened to me so far. They fed me candy and Mt. Dew and I couldn't have been happier.

The room was packed and constantly other visitors were coming and going. I couldn't help but thinking of the way Holly Golightly had described the visits she had with Sally Tomato in Truman Capote's *Breakfast at Tiffany's*. How it was all laughs and fun and then on the way home nobody was either laughing or smiling. In my parent's faces I could see the wear of all the stress they had been under. It was still my fault. I could have prevented all of this. They told me that that week our family had gone on one of their vacations. If I had prevented all of this, the three of us would be joining them. My parents would have been able to go on their anniversary cruise that spring. They would never tell me and to this day they still haven't but I knew that I had ruined a significant chunk of their lives already. Maybe, even, had taken years off of their lives. Tears were welled up in their eyes. The only thing I could do for them is appear as if I was perfectly fine.

Strong in the face of adversity and "Embracing the suck" as I was always so keen to say. And I did just that.

I pretended that I didn't notice their pain. I acted as if the last three months hadn't been the worst of my life. I assured them that this was all temporary, that through Antonio unmasking the counties judicial corruption I would be free before the last frost melted, however, I knew better.

Looking back though, I'm proud of what I did for them. I'm proud that when we had reached the apex of our visit they were jubilant. I was proud that I had cast a facade over that place that made it potentially seem like just my first year at college. Yes, it is true that I felt I had lied by not telling them that I was the living embodiment of a subject to Dante's Inferno. Yes it's true that the dull "blat" sound that a man's head made when it made contact with flesh was still ringing in my ears. And yes, it is true that my head throbbed from the residual stress of all my family's heartache. But if anyone had to truly suffer it was me. If they could leave my visit knowing that their baby was just fine, I would sleep that night with pride in my heart.

My family and my faith was all I had. Bible reading and church three times a week helped my faith. I had to take care of my family. On my walk back I had the Cheshire smile DC once wore. I walked back into the pod, handed my visiting pass back to the CO and he walked me back to my cell.

When I walked in I saw a white pad of paper and a pen on my rack.

One Step Closer

There must have been a mistake. He surely misplaced them. I sat for an hour while he was in his visit trying to decide what to do with them. He came back into the cell just before lunch.

"Hey man, how was your visit?"

He strode in and took off his coat. "It was good, my girl didn't show though."

My heart dropped. "I'm sorry man."

He sat, half looking at his picture of her.

"It's okay, I'm just worried that she's out there using drugs again."

I thought of Ron's similar situation. .

"All we can do is pray, worrying won't help anything."

He nodded but remained silent. Unable to think of anything else to say I remembered the paper.

"Did you leave that for me?" Gesturing toward the pad and pen.

"Yeah, I thought you might be able to use it. You did say you wanted to be a writer."

I smiled, it could have been the nicest thing anyone had done for me since I was first found guilty.

"Thank you, thank you... really."

I picked up the pad gingerly and in the center of the topmost page I wrote "CRC" square in the center. I then started writing down every detail I could remember branching off of it. Some were as simple as one word. Others were as encapsulating as half of a page. The pen was so much better than the "Flexpen" I had used in county. The words were flowing freely onto the page and I was excited too when I would be writing stories, chapters, anything really. When I felt I had finished the "brainweb" I set down the pad and paper and beamed at Kerry.

He had given me so much more than white-lined paper and a "Bic" ballpoint pen, he had given me freedom. I felt more ambitious at rec and decided to take a shower. The downstairs four were full so I walked up the stairs to the top range. To my surprise they were full, too. Not wanting to walk back down to the lower showers and look like I was muling drugs, I stayed in line at the top.

In front of me were two bald men with tattoos covering their faces. The one closest to me had a tattoo covering the back of his head of a blue devil face with the word "Devil" over the top. He turned around, amused.

"Hey, baby face, are you even old enough to be here?"

They both laughed and I laughed along too.

"How old are you, anyways?"

I smiled. "18".

They laughed.

"What did you do at 18 that got you here?"

I told them the story I had told for almost a year. They weren't smiling anymore.

"Wow," said the blue devil. "That's messed up. But you know, I think you're going to get your appeal. I don't see how—"

The other one hushed him. "Come on, man. How often does an appeal actually go through?"

He looked back at him. "It happens, especially with something like that."

He looked back to me "Good luck man, for real."

I thanked them just as they were walking to the two showers that had just opened up. I thought about what the one had said.

"How often does an appeal actually go through—"

"Hey, are you in line?"

I turned around to see a man a few inches taller than me with white hair and glasses.

"Yes."

He stood against the wall and waited with me. I looked back at him.

"How long are you here for?"

He looked up "Two months on an old number."

My brow furrowed. "What do you mean?"

"Parole violation."

I nodded. "Oh, okay. Where are hoping to go?"

He shrugged his shoulders. "I don't care, I can survive anywhere. When I first went for three years I was getting pretty messed up. But I survived and thrived once I joined the Crypts."

I stared at him, unsure whether he was joking or not. Surely this man that looked old enough to be my grandfather and who bore a striking resemblance to an older Sean Connery wasn't a member of a notorious prison gang. Sure enough he outstretched a hand and started to point out his fellow members.

"That's one of my brothers down there, there's another, and one more over there by the ice machine."

The old, skinny white man seemed the exact opposite of all the young, buff black men he pointed out.

"I'm fifty two years old and at some point I decided I wasn't going take the abuse anymore."

I supposed it made sense, though I never would have guessed he was only in his fifties, he looked seventy at least. A door to one of the showers opened and I walked to it. Expecting a warm refreshing shower I was met with a freezing stream with water pressure that turned my skin red. In five minutes I was out and walking back down to my cell. After everyone had locked down I sat on my bunk with the white pad in front of me. The temptation to finally start on the chapters overcame me. I looked down at my outline. I had never wrote more than a couple thousand words at one time in my life, how do you write a book exceeding a hundred pages or more? I sat and silently requested guidance. Almost instantly it was given to me. I enjoyed writing short stories, so if I just wrote each chapter like a short story I could get it all down and not have to worry about it all fitting together until the end. But where was a good place to start? I couldn't write anything about county life until I had my notes to jog my memory. I decided to start when I left county and work toward where I was.

I titled the first white page *No Good at Goodbyes*. I thought back to that day and began.

The wind was rushing past my visor and the cold spring air was seeping through the cracks of my helmet, biting my nose...

Fervidly I wrote. Page by page I stretched it. It was one of the longest short stories I had ever written, though it came so easily. It felt good to recall the events so that I could leave them in the past. Word by word I put down every last detail, desire, and hope and fear I had that day. All the way until I entered the administration building at CRC. When I was done I set down my pen and the small stack of papers on my bed and got up to get a drink. Pensively I looked out the window of my cell into the grass and wire beyond. I felt like I had when I first gave myself to Christ. As if a small weight had been lifted from me. I couldn't wait until I would start the parts where I was actually going through hard times. It would be interesting to say the least. My roommate was still deep in his book so I took the time to pray to Jesus. I knelt down on the cement and closed my eyes.

"Dear Lord. Please forgive me, for I have…"

My eyes opened and I remembered something I had read in Matthew.

"And when you pray, do not heap up empty phrases as the Gentiles do, for they think that they will be heard for their many words.." Matthew 6:7.

I closed my eyes again and uneasily started.

"Dear Jesus, please forgive me for my sins. By sacrificing your life on the cross, which I am eternally grateful, you paved the way that my trespasses may be forgiven. I feel that by knowingly going against your teachings I have soiled the sanctity of everything you do for me. I also acknowledge that I am weak to temptation. Please lead me to do right by you, oh Lord. Help me to be the man you know I can be. Thank you Lord for this wonderful day, thank you for giving me the strength and courage to continue, for allowing me to wake up another day closer to freedom, for my health, and for my incredible family. Please keep them physically safe and mentally strong during these times of tribulation and strife. Help all of us at this compound to work by your example and help us from falling into the lustful grasps of temptation. Lord, I love you. I have faith and belief that you are my lord and savior and that one day I will sit in your father's house to praise his name. Thank you for all of the blessings you have given me and if your will be done please deliver me from this place a well-developed Christian so that I can praise you and spread your teachings all the days of my life.

Our father who art in heaven,
hallowed be thy name,
thy kingdom come,
thy will be done.
On earth as it is in Heaven.
Give us this day our daily bread
and forgive us our trespasses

as we forgive those who trespass against us.
Lead us not from temptation,
but deliver us from evil.
Deliver us, o Lord from every evil and grant us peace in our days.
In your mercy keep us free from sin.
Protect us from all anxiety and worry,
as we wait in joyful hope for the coming of your son, Lord Jesus Christ.
For the kingdom, the power, the glory are yours now and forever.

When I opened my eyes I felt them watery. When I stood I felt light, delicate. Jesus loved me. I could feel it with every breath and every word. And he was right, those meaningless words that I always repeated didn't mean anything. Sure, they sounded good. But the words that I let out that came straight from my heart set my soul free. I wanted to feel this way all of the time. Further, I wanted to tell everyone about this feeling. How amazing it was and how if they accepted Christ with all their being they could also feel this way. I could empathize that I know their pain. I know why they lay up at night, crying, sorrowful as if there is nothing out in the world for them. How every morning is a struggle because they don't want to get up and face a day that will simply beat them down and make them feel worthless.

I wanted to spread the word, help as many as I could. And if God saw fit to leave me at CRC or another parent institution to do it, God's will be done. But if I was able to leave through my appeal or even an appeal bond, I would hit the ground running. I would volunteer at the same places I did before, this time with a message to spread. I would go to youth groups and tell my story, help them to avoid such a terrible future as I faced. Go to churches and spread the gospel that is the true undying faith and love of Christ. There are so many that go to church because they feel like attendance is all it takes to get into heaven. I wanted to go into those places and show them the beauty and the power and the undying glory of God almighty!

Kerry set down his book, "What did you write?"

I told him it was a chapter out of the book I wanted to write and he smiled,

"Well go on then."

I laughed and shook my head. "No... you don't want to hear it, it's not edited or even close to done."

He sat up and looked me straight in the face. "I want to hear it."

Sensing he was genuine I picked up the papers and began to read. At first he laid back, taking in the words. Then as I kept going he sat up and listened attentively. I glanced up, after a joke or a form of symbolism to see his response. He seemed to really like it! I grew more confident and read to the end. When I finished he nodded and smiled.

"I like it!"

At first I thought he was simply being polite, then after further probing I could tell he was being candid. Excited and reassured as to what I was trying to do I stowed the papers and laid down.

That night I fell asleep with a smile on my face, thanking God.

Sparks

Confetti speckled the higher ledges in the huge open common area. Housekeeping had been trying, and failing, for over an hour to clean up the rest of it but to no avail. We came just a week after the new year, it was their "Slow season" indicated by the fact that only thirty five of the six hundred rooms were occupied. I sat in a wooden rocker near a grand fireplace, alternating between watching the dancing flame tongues, the workers up high trying to clean up and looking out the fifty foot tall windows at the far end of the gargantuan A-frame lodge. The lake was frozen all the way across and snow covered the hills and trees surrounding. I exhaled a sigh of strained relief. It was good to be away from that awful town—-

"Wake up!"

The door to our cell was open and our neighbor Travis had his head stuck in. Kerry and I bolted out of our racks, into our shoes and out the door to the already moving lines. Outside the sky was clear, showing the first rays of light in our variegated sky. The crackle of gunfire reverberated off of our compound. I glanced to the thicket of trees at the south end of the camp where the sounds were coming from.

[There must be a shooting range at the corrections officer academy]

With the cold air the crackle carried through the countryside without hardly losing a decibel. Walking to the hall I was met by our neighbor, Travis, shoulder deep in a thick section of bushes. When he emerged he had several small branches in his hair. He quickly and slyly slid back into line. Surprisingly he was not seen by anyone except Kerry and me.

"What was he doing?" I asked Kerry.

Kerry just shrugged his shoulders. "Who knows?"

Oatmeal, juice.

[Breakfast of champions]

Another of our neighbors, "Double back", stood up with an outgoing line and came back in for seconds.

[Who would want more?]

I supposed that in time perhaps I too would crave seconds of stale hardtack and burning hot oatmeal. Walking back in line to our dorm Kerry caught Travis.

"What did you do in the bushes?"

He pulled out a wad of wet chewing tobacco from his pocket. My stomach turned at the long cut discarded wad.

"I'm gonna sell it."

This was definitely something new.

"How are you selling it?" asked Kerry

"What do you mean?"

He sounded genuinely confused.

"I'm going to dry it out, roll it into five or six cigarettes and sell it."

[Remind me not to buy cigarettes.]

"No, No, No, No. You should throw it in a bag with some water so it gets fresh again and sell it as chew."

I couldn't believe the conversation I was hearing.

"Nah, bro. I could sell that for, four bucks? If I roll it I can easily get ten dollars from the rolls."

[Only a convict can look at discarded chew in a bush and turn it into ten dollars.]

He seemed to have won the discussion walking into my dorm I saw a teabag hanging from a tree.

[this is the weirdest college...]

When I came back to my cell I found a Kite on the ground. It was the one I had sent to the public defender. When I opened it, it read

Mr. McGail, as you know, Mr. Bueti filed your appellate paperwork on 10/9/14. Any questions regarding your appeal should be addressed to him. Good luck!

[Psssh, luck. Who needs luck when you have Jesus?]

I felt a slight twinge of doubt flick across my mind. Suppressing it, I turned my mind to my proverbs. The day's message was not to affiliate or wish to be with evil men.

[I should have started reading proverbs long ago.]

Thinking back, I remembered my dad warning me about them. I never could have imagined that not listening to my dad would put me in a state penitentiary. I mean, they seemed nice enough.

[I suppose that they were-]

"-and I don't think it sounds very good. Were you listening at all?"

I frowned and shook my head.

"No, I'm sorry."

He looked at me for a second then started over.

"I said, can you please look over the letter I am sending in with my judicial? I wrote it up early last night."

He looked at me with a patient mix of inquiry and agitation from my previous inattention.

"Um…yeah, sure. I can't promise I'll be a huge help but I can try."

His face lit up. "Thanks!"

He dug in his box briefly and pulled out a judicial packet that he had wrote on. Reading it over, I noticed minor spelling and grammatical errors but nothing that was obviously invalid about it.

"I'm going to mull it over during lunch and do it before dinner, okay?" he nodded his assent.

I laid the paper down and rested my head for a mid-morning nap.

Dawn. The first rays of sunlight were ablaze in the east, setting the sky aflame. I sat in the grass between the barn and the field watching the glorious orb rise over the town that wished my ultimate destruction. A cigarette hung between my fingers, smoke ascending into the sky. The brightly collared glass pipe lay in the damped grass beside me. Half of the contents green, half black. I indulged in it so rarely those days, though after thirteen hours behind my computer screen readying myself for the week of classes ahead and studiously scanning every line of the "discovery" packets for my trial, I felt I had earned a break. The red bull and caffeine pills I had taken were only now being dulled by the pot I had smoked. No longer did I feel like my heart was going to explode. Now, with the sun warming my face and the nicotine refreshing my senses I balanced precariously between the vices of catatonia and tachycardia. While in this brief state I admired the unparalleled beauty of where I had lived for many years. Even as I walked a tightrope with freedom and success in front of me and the judicial warlord below me I had the final realization that life is beautiful. Though tribulation and tumult drags one down the world's astonishing beauty can uplift you out of even the deepest pit. And in this moment, as the early morning fog rolled from the plains, I sat. Taking a last drag from the stick I had long chastised my mother for using I buried the remaining tobacco in the ground and pocketed the filter. The glass of the pipe was wet and although still warm I lugged it in my pocket back to my house where fresh coffee was waiting to welcome me.

My eyes fluttered open and I could hear the radio from the pod officers at their desk.

"B-2, B-3; break and hold."

I know that because they were now being ordered to line up for chow, we were soon to follow. Kerry was reading his Bible and I slowly put on my blue shirt, coat and shoes. Before too long we were walking in our lines to chow. With the sun high in the sky and a light breeze blowing from the west I couldn't help but think back to my dream. How funny it was that now, nearly six months later I was still using a "Bic" to spark my release.

Though now I was using ink instead of a lighter, lined paper instead of rolling paper, God instead of ganja. How long it had taken me to realize what I truly wanted out of life. And at what cost? I had lost so much, yet I was still happy. I was still alive. I still understood, looking up at the sparsely clouded blue sky that life is beautiful.

And not in a "Mr. Brainwash", consumerism kind of way. But in a pure, beautiful, natural way. I floated in zealous exaltation back to the dorm after chow and lay down. How different I was now in comparison to the person I was a year, six months, even two weeks before. My changing was rising in a crescendo of maturity and strength.

…when I was a child, I spoke like a child, I thought like a child, I reasoned like a child. When I became a man, I gave up childish ways… 1 Corinthians 13:11

Before I knew it we were in our lines walking back to the block. I could remember something my dad said about basic training. The whole time he felt like he was either marching to chow, waiting in line for chow or marching from chow. I guess I could say the same about my situation. Soon I felt my bed rise up and meet me as I jumped down onto it.

With a sigh of near pure bliss I sat up and began writing Kerry's judicial letter on a fresh sheet of paper. Each letter I carefully wrote, trying desperately to write in a legible way as opposed to my usual physician script. When I was done I handed it to him. As he read his nod grew increasingly exaggerated and when he set it down he smiled at me.

"Thank you so much!"

I felt blood rush to my face. "No don't thank me. It's still you writing I just changed some stuff around and respelled a couple words here and there."

He looked at me with playful indignation. "Oh, come on. It sounds really, really good. And even though the judge already told me he wasn't going to grant my judicial, I think I'm gonna get it."

I smiled in spite of myself. "Well, you're welcome."

The CO's voice boomed: "Get ready for rec!"

I jumped up and grabbed my JPay number, excited that I could finally log on after registering nearly a week prior. When my door clicked open I raced to the TV room and there was already at least 10 people in line. I took a seat and patiently waited. Slowly but surely over the course of an hour and a half each person in line (and some not in line) got on JPay. When I got on, finally, I had a message from my dad testing the system and money on my commissary books. When I went back into my cell after rec I felt excited that I had had such a good day. Sitting down I noticed the pad of white paper on my box "Calling" to me. I felt that with such a good day behind me I could finish it off right by writing another chapter.

I chuckled to myself. It felt juvenile to think that these stories could muster up enough substance to create a tangible, likable story. Nonetheless I titled the second chapter *709871*.

As I wrote I felt myself fumbling back to the first day I was at CRC. It was amazing how far I had come in such a short time. When I finished and set down the last page Kerry was looking at me expectantly

"Well…"

I knew what he was hinting at but played along.

"Well....what?"

He sighed, exasperated. "Well are you going to read it?"

Once again I hesitated. Before being locked up I had only let one person read through my writings. A girl nonetheless.

"I don't kn—"

"Don't give me that. Let's hear it!"

I grunted my displeasure and read to him the second chapter. Part of the way through Travis's head poked in the window with a cigarette in hand.

"You guys want to buy one?" We looked at each other.

Kerry spoke first. "What would I do with that? I can't' even light it."

He shrugged. "Whatever man." He disappeared from the window.

"Do people really buy those?"

Kerry nodded. "I would have if I could light it."

Shortly after we heard a "click" outside in the pod and one of the lights flickered. I kept reading and another "click" interrupted me.

"What is that?"

Kerry shook his head. "Probably Travis popping the circuit."

Taken aback I asked "What? How did he get out? How's he doing it?"

He sat up and put his feet on the floor.

"His cellie is a porter so his door is always unlocked. And he probably has two staples sticking out of an eraser with a piece of pencil lead connecting them. When he sticks the staples in the outlet the lead turns red hot and then he lights a piece of toilet paper on fire and lights the roll-up."

Click. "Dammit!"

Kerry laughed, "It doesn't seem like he's getting it."

"Click Click."

"Hey!" echoed the familiar tunes of a CO.

"You fucking moron! Why would you do that right in front of me!? Well, you better hope the camera didn't see you, lock down you idiot."

Kerry and I broke into laughter. I could just picture him sitting cross legged on the floor sticking a pencil with staples sticking out of the eraser into the electrical outlet while a cigarette was hanging out of his mouth. And, when accosted looking up as if nothing's wrong and saying "What?"

What surprised me more than anything, though, was that the CO didn't seem to care as long as his boss didn't see. When I finished reading the chapter to Kerry we laid down and listened to arguments between the CO and Travis:

"Stop smoking where I can see you!"

"I'm not smoking!"

When I woke up the next morning I could still smell the lingering odors of tobacco. I looked at the folder on the wall and saw the kite I wrote a day before still waiting to be turned in. I took it and shoved it in my pocket. It was a request to see the law library. I felt more and more like I should complete my own individual research. I felt the folds of the kite and sat down to put my shoes on for chow.

First Encounters

"Are you affiliated with a gang?" She looked at me with a practiced patience.

"No." I laughed slightly though I knew that by saying no I was once again the minority.

"What happened?" I paused, curiously analyzing the question.

"What do you mean?"

She shifted in her seat and repeated the question unyielding. "What happened?"

Slowly it dawned on me that her inquiry was pertaining to my case. I slowly enumerated the same events I had been detailing for a year. When I was finished she peered at me over her glasses. Turning the wedding ring on her finger she spoke. "So, if that's the case how can you be here?"

I nodded in agreement. "I asked myself that same question for quite some time. To be honest a healthy mix of prosecutor and juror misconduct had a good amount to do with it. Because of which I am fairly confident with an appeal…"

She adjusted the collar of her white sweater and sat silent for a moment. The silence in the TV room was so great that I could hear her feet racking back and forth on the floor beneath the table in the space that separated us.

"Oh..." Her voice was a whisper. We looked at each other for a brief moment and I noted the sad, contemplative look in her eye. I looked away, nervous. She cleared her throat, straightened her relaxed posture and regained her professional demeanor. "In the past, have you generally found yourself running from fights, avoiding them but somehow they find you, or, do you look for them?"

I smiled sadly, "I've never been in a fight."

She scribbled on her paper [Runs from]. "Okay, if you wanted to get someone to do something how would you do it?"

I frowned. "Like to do me a favor?"

She tapped her pen on the table. "No; like something they shouldn't do, or, might not want to do. How would you get them to do it?"

I had to think. Was there ever a time that I had done that? She stared at me patiently. After contemplating I did remember one occasion. "Well, when I want to get my three-year-old niece to eat her vegetables I always have her think it's her idea. I suppose that's what I would do."

She nodded, satisfied and wrote something else on her paper. "Well, Patrick. That will do. I am going to enter your score into the computer and it will generate your classification. Thank you."

I stood up and smiled, "Thank you, Anita." When I walked to her to shake her hand I noticed her face slightly flushed. I gave her a firm yet gentle handshake and told her to have a nice day as I left the room. Crossing the pod back to my cell I glanced back towards her. She was sitting at the table again reading over the notes while turning her necklace in her fingers. She looked back toward me through the windows noticing my gaze. I looked away and walked to my cell embarrassed.

Back in my cell I sat down, ready for my first outside rec and thinking back to the way she had looked at me when I had told my story. *[I couldn't do that job]* I thought, thinking about all the stories she must have heard every day. I wondered how she did it, how she scrubbed the thoughts from her mind when she returned home so that she could become just another normal person again. But then, I thought, maybe she couldn't. Maybe working in those unholy hollow halls left an imprint on every person's soul that tried to leave. Forever you would be imprinted by the garbage disposal of society.

One thing I noticed that was exactly like every prison movie I had ever seen was the yard. Twenty men crowded the area where the pull-up and dip bars were. Shirtless and covered with tattoos they did harder workouts than some pararescue men and army rangers I had met. Two basketball courts were hosts to "Shirt vs Skin" games of basketball. *[No fouls called here, I see.]* A volleyball court lay disheveled after what must have been years of poor maintenance. A group of horseshoe pits bordered the far side of the basketball courts, players used non-metal horseshoes. Two football fields and two handball courts were also left deserted whether because of violent games or lack of supplies I didn't know. Sets of picnic tables were set up by the horseshoe pits and the pull-up jumbo bars and a quarter mile track circled the assorted fields and courts.

After a small number of short sets on the pull-up/dip bars I elected to walk the track and enjoy the beautiful weather while it lasted. The track on the far side came within 10 feet of the fence which was closer than I had been to it since I first got there. I looked up and admired the great lengths that the constructor had taken to ensure that nobody could enter or exit. In addition to the two fences, razor wire and gravel there were cement foundations to stop anyone from tunneling under the fences and motion activated trip wire weaved through the inner fence. There was an actual science to keeping humans in cages that was for sure. After walking slightly over a mile the yard was called to reform our lines and we walked back to our cellblock.

"Hey Patrick." I looked around the lines for who called my name. "Yo, Patrick." I met eyes with the man with the face tattoos I saw on TV at county.

"Hey, man. You know who I am?" I nodded my assent.

"I heard you took care of my bro at county."

"Once again I nodded "yeah, he's pretty cool. Do you know what he got?" He seemed surprised I talked "Yeah, he got a year. Hey we're heading in, I'll holler at you later."

The top range line walked back into the pod leaving me in the bottom range waiting. I knew that treating the kid right would pay off. *I can't imagine where I'd be if I took his trays....* walking inside a young white kid in front of me leaned down and picked up a small plastic bundle that fell out of his pant leg. It looked like white powder wrapped into a section of trash bag no larger than a strawberry. He picked it up and looked around hastily to make sure nobody had seen him. Satisfied, he walked on, putting the ball into the front of his pants.

"Is there cocaine here too?"

Kerry turned toward me; "yes, why do you ask?"

I looked across the block, looking at all of the faces, all of the different backgrounds, all of the different corners of society lumped together in the same blue uniforms. "Oh, no reason. How much does that kind of stuff go for?"

He shrugged. "I don't really know. I've never messed with it." I could only imagine the heaven my former Codefendant was in at Lebanon with all the drugs and cheap tattoos he could want.

It was Midsummer. The warm breeze carried through the rising cornfield to where we sat. Graced by such a wonderful day my brother and his girlfriend sat with our sister, niece and I as we passed the time talking. Indistinct laughter could be heard from the field. Standing up I elected to check on the younger girls playing. From my vantage point I could see a front loader sitting just within the group of corn stocks. A young, and unidentifiable girl was waving me to come, quick. I ran over to find my youngest niece lying Unconscious under the bucket of the front loader in a pile of corn stocks. I called for my brother to come help as I sifted through the pile of broken crops to get to her. He ran over and took the other girl away. I looked up at my niece and started running her back to the house. "Call 911!" I yelled to my sister. Regaining my common sense I checked her pulse it was there and I checked her breathing, bilateral and steady she was okay.

I woke up in a cold sweat. The lights were still off and Kerry was still asleep and snoring. I set up on my rack and ran my hands through my hair. What had brought that dream on? Usually, as of recent I had been dreaming almost exclusively of vacations or trips I took with my family and almost always the dreams I had were true events. This was neither. I hadn't worried about the girls in weeks and yet now I was terrified. Something bad and imminent was going to happen to them. I prayed with my eyes filling with tears that God would protect them from any and all harm. I stayed awake the rest of the night. The weekend went by in a blur of meals sleep and two more nightmares about my nieces. The dreams were both similar in that I was trying to get them out at my parents' house while it was burning down.

Monday morning came and my parents, brother, and lawyer had a visit. I felt that it was better not to talk about my dreams and instead filled them in on everything I had noticed there At CRC so far and how my roommate was professing himself and writing a "how to " guide to beginning Christian. When he asked me to copy it I took it as he wanted me to proofread it much like his judicial packet. When he read the copies he was upset that I change the Lord's words being channeled through him and wanted me to rewrite it verbatim. As kindly as I could I told him I wasn't right for the job. Disheartened he decided that instead he would just pay to use the camps copy machine.

My lawyer took me aside and told me briefly the major pillars of our appeal case. Before he left I remembered my mom told me in the visit previously that I could sue the prosecutor for severing attorney-client privilege. Asking him if he could look into the probability of our success he said he would get back to me. When he left my family and I continued to talk for the remaining five hours when I left I was sad that I couldn't see them for another week or more but was ready to go to the law library and research case studies in relation to our appeal premises.

Back at my cell I found the pass for the law library I had requested that Friday when I heard my lawyer was coming. I didn't bother to close my door. I turned and headed back outside for the library, thanking God for such wonderful happenings. The law library was a broom closet no larger than a standard bedroom. There were three computers set up on one side, three on the other and a series of tables were in the center. Shelves on the walls held volumes of books on evidence, contracts, Ohio revised code, federal sentencing, federal procedure and a wide array of obscure legal references. A man sitting at the first computer greeted me as did a half grown pit bull. I petted the dog and looked up at the cadre worker.

"Can I help you?"

I produced my pass. "Yes I have a pass to come here, I am interested in researching case studies pertaining to my appeal."

He nodded. I could hear an NPR show was playing from the tape player. "Has your lawyer filed a notice of appeal?" The dog was lapping water from a bowl beside me.

"Yes."

He motioned to a computer. "Okay are you familiar with Lexis Nexis?"

I shook my head and shrugged. "Nope."

He turned on the monitor. "It's not overly complicated, just type In the tag you wish to search, say, juror misconduct. And it shows up here." 800 cases with the outcomes clearly stated appeared.

"Okay, thank you." I sat down and began typing for cases.

- Not giving mistrial - 400 results
- Forced to testify from testimony given - 150 results
- Testifying on testimony not given - 38 results
- Withholding interviews - 75 results
- Seizing file - 0 results
- Seizing file from defendant - 0 results
- Severing attorney client privilege - 1 result

After an hour and a half searching I found the closest thing to what I wanted. When the defendant's original lawyer divulged attorney-client privilege information he was sued by the defendant. Case resulted in the relief of $11 million. I stared at the screen with my mouth agape and reread the line over and over again. ....11 million. My heart skipped a beat, my breath was held and I couldn't remember putting a banana in my pocket. The 30s man with a receding hairline and beard came over to me as I was logging off.

"Anything else I can help you with?" I began to shake my head then remembered the case study I couldn't find.

"Yes, actually " He sat down next to me and listened intently.

"Well, I couldn't find any case study regarding a prosecutor seizing the file of the defendant from counsel. What would I search for that?"

He sat back, shocked. "I'm not sure I understand." He hesitated. "You mean, they took **your** file from…"

"My attorney, yes."

He sat forward, pointedly "I'm not sure that has ever happened before your case."

I looked at him with surprise. He looked at my computer screen for a moment then returned to his desk.

I idly browsed Lexis Nexis while looking out the windows to where the cadre lived. They walked around, laughed, ran on the track and just plain lived. Again I couldn't believe how incredibly similar the institution was to a college campus. It was not at all a damp dungeon, though at the same time it wasn't the shining example of rehabilitation I supposed it should have been. It was in a strange middle ground where humanity and the continuance of attitudes resided. There was no guard brutality or outright abuse though the dorms and buildings were like palimpsests of the past abuses long covered up with a veneer of statutory humanity. I wondered how many people were innocent, how many could be easily swayed from crime but were now stuck in the facsimile of redemption. Before I knew it I had to leave the law library and I walked through the regular library, which was not much larger, then towards my block with the cool Autumn air whipping across my face.

Love and Marriage

Kerry was lightly snoring when I returned to the cell. On his locker box was a new book, *Darwinism Under the Microscope*, I smiled and sat down with it. Outside a light rain fell in the fields. A piece of paper slid underneath the cell door. Walking over to it I saw the masthead.

Department of Rehabilitation & Corrections.
Name: Patrick McGail.

I froze, staring at the folded piece of paper on the floor. Slowly I picked it up, pulled the staple away and unfolded it.

Patrick McGail
Classification: 3
Institution: Warren Correctional Institution.

[not CRC cadre] I read the paper several more times. A second piece of paper slid under the door. I picked it up and sat back on my rack.

"Grmph…. wassit. Wassit say?" Mustered Kerry from his cocoon.

"Um…my classification papers."

His head emerged from the covers. "To CRC cadre? You should be gone by tomorrow morning."

I shook my head, eyes glued to the page. "No, I'm going to Warren."

His eyes opened and he sat up. "I'm sorry, at least you are leaving here, though."

I nodded, apprehensive and laid-back wondering what this new "home" had in store for me. The day dragged on with my growing worries. Every time I saw somebody I knew I asked what Warren was like. And from everybody I got the same responses.

"It's cool there."

"You'll do fine."

"Good luck."

I cringe when I heard "good luck." From what I had surmised, Warren was next to the worst prison in Ohio, Lebanon. It acted as an "honor camp" for the larger "Leb". When the people who were violent enough to go to Leb got good behavior they went to Warren, which, as far as I could tell, was good and bad because on one hand at least I wasn't going to Leb, "knife camp". But on the other hand I had to leave the place I had grown comfortable with and go to a real prison where, as Sickmann would say, they "fuck boys and get money." To that day I didn't know what that meant and I didn't want to find out.

The day turned into the night and before I knew it I was lying in the dark still silence. I prayed over and over that I could stay at CRC at least until Monday so I can see my dad and brother again. Minutes swept into hours as I lay restless in the dark. I reached below me and my cup of water and instead found my book. Pity I still had 70 pages left. I tossed it at my feet and laid back once again with anxieties rising. Kerry's breathing had deepened, he was asleep. I wondered what time it was. Tossing around the bed I knocked the book to the floor. I picked it up and lay it in my lap. Perhaps it would be better to read than just soak in my worries. Loosening my grip on the binding the pages opened up to my bookmark. I scooted my back down to where the thin sliver of light fell on my bed. Soon enough, I cleared my mind and was enthralled in the story. Pages flew by and every time I began to feel tired I made a cup of instant coffee from the sink and continued on. Determined to finish before I left, I pressed on later into the night. Time was measured only by the occasional CO flashlight check shining in the cell. One… Two… Three. I judged by my third cup of coffee that coincided with the third check that it was around two in the morning. I sat down and pressed on. Page upon page I continued until finally it was gone. It had been five hourly flashlight checks when I laid down on top of my covers, thoroughly satisfied with the work on the book and the phenomenal ending. I hoped that I would have a similar reuniting with my family outside prison like the heroine. Thanking God for helping me finish the book, leading me to the inspiration, I fell fast asleep.

"Knock Knock! McGail." My eyes fluttered. "McGail, McGail" the soft tones of her voice roused me. I looked up to see a stunning woman CO. "McGail –" she said "pack it up, you're leaving." I sat up and smiled weakly, her incredible features reminded me of Esperanza Spalding. She left the door cracked and walked off. I suppose that she left to practice her standing bass. I stood and slowly began filling my laundry bag with my clothes, sheets , and commissary. I tucked my two Bibles gingerly in the bottom and placed other items around them to keep from disturbing them in transit. Kerry hadn't stirred and once again I felt that compulsion to leave without saying goodbye. I slipped the letter I wrote him in his Bible and made my way towards the door.

"Still not good at goodbyes?" I smiled and turned to face him, now standing.

"I suppose not." He returned the smile and shook my hand.

"You will do fine. Just keep God close. If the Lord is for you, who can be against you."

I thanked him and asked him to write. He agreed and laid back on his mat. Walking out of the cell I thanked God for such an amazing bunkie and hoped to be lucky again. The air outside was icy with a strong wind sweeping through the compound. Walking to the chow hall with the other two ride-outs from my area I recognized that the only other pod present in the hall was R unit. It was Thursday. So many of them had shaved heads looking around nervously. I chuckled and nudged the person in front of me.

"Funny, you can tell the new ones by sight."

He grimaced. "I can smell their fear from here."

I made a mental note not to talk to him again. Grits, eggs, milk, bread. Before I had a chance to shovel all the food down we were called out. Following the others with my laundry bag over my shoulder we made our way to the building marked "Intake, release." Walking the halls I couldn't help but remember my first day nervously looking around as if someone would jump out at any moment and stab me with a toothbrush. We, 57 in all, filed into the hallway near where we first entered. The CO had us separate by the compound we were going. Lebanon on the left, Chillicothe on the right, Warren in holding cell "A", Ross in holding cell "B." I walked into the holding cell and there were only seven of us. Nobody looked familiar but a portly, tattooed white kid approached me.

"First number?"

I nodded, "Can you tell?"

He smiled and patted me—more swatted me—on the back. "You'll do fine, White."

I reacted, "What?"

He stared then smiled again. "My name is White."

I laughed. "Ohhh, haha. How did you get that nickname?" He seemed less and less interested in the conversation.

"I was the only white kid in my hood." He walked away to greet an inmate with full face and head tattoos. I sat in the vaulted holding cell wondering what my family was doing right then. Was my Dad sitting at his desk peering over large spectacles while typing away on an ergonomic keyboard? Was my brother at the skate park pondering quantum mechanics and the practical uses of his Raspberry Pi's? Was my sister learning about a new religion from part of the world that I had never heard of or chasing her daughters around the house? Was my Mom pontificating the idiocrasy of modern technology while simultaneously completing twice her workload and holding the financial burden of Ohio's Civil Air Patrol on her shoulders using an out of date windows computer and a last-season high performance laptop? I sighed, intellectual stimulation or even basic human conversations were a rarity those days. The only chance I had at happiness was the fifteen minute phone calls, two hour visitations and the postage shoved underneath my door. Outside of that the only solace I —

"Hey, Patrick." I looked up, unaware that the heavily tattooed kid had walked up to me.

"Um…hi, do I know you?" He sat down next to me and turned toward me revealing a large white scar running the length of his head.

"Yeah, I'm Jiminy. Remember? Well, anyways I just wanted to let you know that there are no hard feelings."

I hesitated. "No hard—"

He cut in seamlessly "for killing my cousin."

I let out my breath. "Oh", I tensely started "…no, no, no I didn't kill him." He looked me dead in the eye. "You were just there, then?"

I sighed and recounted the events just as I had for the year prior. When I finished he nodded and said solemnly. "I knew there was something funny about those guys. He nudged the plump white kid, White. "Make sure you watch out for him. Make sure he doesn't get into anything he shouldn't."

I asked him "Where are you going?"

He smiled. "I'm going back to Leb." White gave a sound of pure jealousy. With that Jiminy walked off with his chin high and an ever knowing smile. The next two hours brought more waiting and trying to force conversation with White to try and make at least one friend where I was going. Finally our group was called out of the now packed room and into another room with tables numbered one through six. We each walked to one of the tables. A CO behind each table, emptied our respective bags onto the tables and inventoried everything we had.

- 3 undershirts
- 3 pairs of socks
- 3 undershorts
- 1 pair shoes (black)
- 1 pair shower shoes
- 1 toothbrush holder

- 1 one shampoo
- 1 toothbrush
- 2 cups
- 1 deodorant
- 1 box tea
- 1 bottle hot sauce
- 1 bottle ear drops
- 2 stamped envelopes
- 3 legal tablets
- assorted pictures
- letters (assorted)
- papers (assorted)
- 1 container oatmeal
- 14 Ramen noodle soups
- 1 Bible

When he was done sifting through my property for any contraband he threw away my calendar I had found in B1 and shoved everything else in a 55 gallon garbage bag.

"Go into the hallway, throw your property into the bin labeled 'WCI' with the property slip facing out so WCI is visible, go back into the holding cell, pick a pair of orange shoes that fit, come back out into the hallway and wait with your group." I was still trying to tie shut my bag when I was ushered out of the room by a large CO with a beard. Trying to remember what the instructions were I stood in the hallway.

"What the fuck are you doing?! Are you deaf, dumb, blind or stupid?! You can't follow directions?! You think that because you're leaving you can do whatever you want?! Put the damn bag in the bin—" He threw my bag in the bin. "Get a God damned pair of shoes." I grabbed the largest available and rushed back into the hallway.

"Get on the wall." I squeezed between White and a seven foot tall Ethiopian man. "Now that he's got his shit together, everyone here going to WCI?" We all nodded. "Good, as I walk down the line hand me your ID and take all of your clothes off and lay them in front of you." Three more CO's walked in front of the seven of us once we were stark naked. "Open your mouths, lift your tongue, pull down your lower lip, now the upper lip, pull you mouth wide, show the bottoms of your hands, raise your arms up, lean your heads forward and shake out your hair, now your beards, turn around, grab your ankles, cough, spread your cheeks, stand up, put on your socks, now your underwear, put on your undershirt, now the orange jumpsuits on the ground, put on the orange slip on shoes, zip up the jump suits, get back on the wall and don't make a sound."

I wondered if I hadn't gone to prison if I would have known what it was like to have no rights. In groups of two they had us kneel on the two black chairs where they handcuffed us arm in arm and shackled our feet. The only person without a partner was White. While I waddled next to the enormously tall black man White walked casually behind.

"Get comfortable, boys. This is going to be an intimate two hour ride. Love and Marriage!" He echoed the sound and the six of us mumbled our displeasure.

"Love and Marriage, Love and Marriage!" We stopped short of a large bin labeled "WCI". While we waited a large man with a button up shirt and belt walked up to the bin to sort the bags. The inmate number on his back and the wear of his uniform indicated he had been in prison a while.

"Hey, Old School". White walked to the front of the line. "What's up?" He glanced toward him but only shrugged his shoulders. "How long have you been down?"

"Thirty-five in December"

White whistled. "Daaaamn. I bet your bunkie loves you. What do you got? Probably a TV, radio, JP4, guitar——"

"I don't have a bunkie."

The tall man beside me looked over. "Are you on restriction?"

He nodded quickly, trying to stay focused on his work. A bald white man near the front of the line joined the barrage.

"Why? Did you beat one up or something?" He shook his head.

"No…No…5—" Another piped in "are you gay or something?"

He mumbled to himself then said "No, Ooh…killed two cellies in the past."

"Bullshit!" one said.

126

"I don't believe it" said another.

"Man you perpin like a mother" said my companion.

"Why did you do it?" asked White.

He shrugged. "I didn't like them. I told the CO's not to give me a cellie and I told the bastards when they came in to move out or I would kill them. They didn't move out so I stabbed one in the throat while he was sleeping and bashed the other's head in on the toilet."

I felt sick. I didn't know whether to believe him and be afraid or not believe him and wonder why he really had a restriction on cellies. Before I had a chance to think about it much further we started walking toward the door I first entered at the correctional reception center. On the way out we passed an inmate in a wheelchair with no legs telling the CO next to him:

"I would beat that bitch down all over again, too Fuck this time, it ain't shit but free meals and a warm bed."

It was raining when we walked outside. The mist with the wind felt like tiny rocks hitting you in the face. We walked past a large tan school bus with metal grating on all of the windows and up to a small sheriff van behind it. By the time we were sitting in the van we all were damp from the rain and piled on top of each other. Regardless, within ten minutes of pulling away from the main gate I was asleep sitting straight up, the Ethiopian on my left side snoring and White on my right talking loudly about how he was going to...

"fuck around and stab a mother fucker so that I can get back to Leb where I belong."

B

Warren Correctional Institute loomed in the distance. A huge monument to the indiscretions of the morally inadequate. Four huge three tier arms branched off of the titanic central building.

"Wow" I whispered. "It's huge."

White looked at me with a whimsical grin." That's Lebanon, dumb ass, that's Warren." He pointed to a lower spot of the hill Leb was on to a small camp of red brick buildings held within barbed wire.

I was elated. "Oh, well that's not so bad."

White sighed." Yeah, it's so small. I miss Lebanon."

I looked over to see him pensively staring out the window. How long has it been since you were there?"

He shrugged and said "9 months." The words left his mouth reminiscent of a school girl telling her friend of the boy she missed. Pulling up to the gates I checked the time on the dashboard. Count was being performed. For an hour and a half we waited. A thin layer of smoke was blowing about the car from the exhaust outside. With the circulation feature activated in the cab of the van we were seven men in a CO_2 gas chamber. Twenty minutes after the engine had filled our cabin, making us gag and cough, praying for a quick death we were sitting in an intake room. A prevention video for rape was playing without sound while we were moved around the intake room, collecting our new uniforms, receiving our room assignments and taking in the refreshingly complaisant correction officers. When we moved about they didn't rush us or toy with their handcuffs preparing to take us to the hole. They sat with us and as long as we didn't defecate on the floor or put a foreign object in one another they wouldn't even raise their voices. They took our long toothbrushes that we had and gave us inch long stubs. Supposedly the year before they had a terrible problem with knives in the prison. I thought to myself that the toothbrush they gave me would make a nicer knife than the one they had taken. Once our long toothbrushes were taken and we all had our housing assignments we were told to file out and follow the obtuse CO who had completed our intake. We passed by the pod reserved for the criminally insane where two of our party walked in to find their new homes among those who danced the thorazine shuffle. We then walked out of the administration building and onto the yard.

The buildings looked the same as the ones from the correctional reception center. The only difference was the hillier landscape. We were led across the yard to the medical building. Sitting inside we were each told to wait to see the nurse in the lobby until our numbers were called, then we would go to get our blood pressure taken before an "official" medical examination. We sat and waited. After an hour we were brought lunches from the chow hall. After another hour we began to protest the new comers seeing the doctor before us. A half hour later I was sitting on a paper covered table before a skeptical doctor who didn't seem to believe anything I had to say. When I returned to the lobby White was talking to an interesting looking man who had an air of absolute certainty to him and a very alluring smile that made you want to believe anything and everything he said. He told us his name was "B". He told us about the drug and violence situations at the camp, how the CO's coordinated searches and to White's request detailed the different gangs at the camp. He stopped when a stringy man with a nervous walk came in. B immediately stopped what he was talking about and went over to him. They argued quietly at first then with a shattering of speckled loud words I could just make out that they were arguing about a knife. Apparently one that the string man was supposed to have held. B had either made or bought it and string man was supposed to hold on to it while B was preparing to do whatever he was going to do with it. Unfortunately, before he could give it back he was discovered by the police and lost B's property. The outcome of the argument was that string man had to pay the fifteen dollars for the lost knife as well as, what I perceived to be punitive damages, an additional five dollars. When their talk had ceased and B had given string man a list of goods to get him at the commissary to amend his fault B walked back over to us and sat down. He sat in silence briefly then looked to me and spoke.

"What's your name?"

I told him and he thought about this for a second.

"What are you here for?"

I looked him in the eye and sighed.

"Two people broke into a house to rob a drug dealer, while they were trying to rob him something went wrong and the one guy shot and killed him. They think I was one of the people in the house."

I continued to account everything that had happened with my case and even at CRC all the way up to sitting on the wood bench next to him. Again he thought about this and reached out for my ID on my jacket. With it in hand he wrote down my name and number on a small piece of paper with my pen. He handed back my ID and pen and in reaction to my expression told me that he had a lot of friends in 3-B and would make sure they took care of me.

When the last person came back from the office we all left to go to our respective housing. White, B and I walked together to the brick building attached to 3A. He shook my hand and White and I walked into the steel doors. The first thing I noticed was the noise. The acoustics could pick up a penny dropped from across the room and eighty men talking noisily was nothing except deafening. The thing I remember most vividly was how dark the walls, floor, and ceiling in the room were, of course creating an overall darker setting, while there was still a flood of natural light from the behemoth windows in the upper range. We walked in our new intake white uniforms past the inhabitants of our new home. The CO in the block led us to a room where they had put our assigned mats. White and I each grabbed one and walked back into the day room where I got a good look at my new surroundings. Two ranges of cells linked a huge common area filled with metal tables, two pillars on opposing sides of the day room with phones and the state's finest degenerates. Walking to one of the stair cases I was beckoned over to one of the steel doors. Inside the inhabitants, a fit black man with tight cropped hair and a slim white man with long brown hair had hung a blanket over their window making the cell near pitch black. When I looked inside all I could make out at first was the glow of the TV in the corner. When my eyes adjusted I could see the white man standing just back from the door. He moved forward and spoke through the crack between the door and the stop.

"How do you know B?"

I thought for a second and answered back through the crack

"We met in the medical, he's pretty sweet."

I regretted my wording right away but my correspondent seemed to understand my meaning.

"Alright, well he sent in a scribe and told us to look out for you. Holler at me at Rec, we need to talk."

I nodded and started walking toward the stairs. Again, I was stopped by a short, fit man with dark skin and glasses.

"Are you Pat?"

I nodded.

"B stated to look out for you so if you need anything I'm just a few doors down. Names Walter."

I extended a quick thank you and started to move up the stairs before I would lose grip of my mat and mesh bag. With belongings slipping from my grip I saw White standing in front of a door ajar. I walked to him and followed him into the cell. Like the first cell I saw the new one had a blanket on the window. The only man in the four man cell had a chest full of hard tattoos and stood easily at Seven feet tall. The cell smelled lightly of reefer and the tall man was swaying around the cell with music blasting out of clear CL-20 style headphones. When I put my mat on the bottom of one of the two bunks and sat down I looked around for the first time at my surroundings. The cell was in the shape of a truncated triangle with a porcelain toilet and sink near the door.

"Did you just arrive from CRC?"

"Yes."

"Have you been to the quartermaster?"

"No." It was no matter, within a couple days we would go and receive our new uniforms so we wouldn't have to be in the oh-so-obvious whites.

"Is this your first number?"

" It is mine."

" Why are you so quiet?

"I am usually fairly reserved, No? Reclusive, still? I keep to myself."

"Are you here for a sex crime?"

"No, it is not a sexual case that I am here for. I am relieved you don't judge but it's not."

What are you reading?

"An article on prosecutorial misconduct. My dad sent it."

"Are you going to appeal?"

"Yes, I am going to appeal. Are you doing a lot of time?"

"No, I really do not have that much time. My name is Todd, I am going to look after you. I can tell you aren't really meant to be here. I am leaving in a couple of months, but I'll make sure you're taken care of when I'm gone."

Rec was a building on the North end connected to a chapel. There was a workout room and basketball court. The white man from my arrival was John. John B. He "held the keys" in the block for a gang called the Cincinnati white boys. Despite its name the group was bi racial. Actually, it apparently was not so much a gang as a family. Regardless of whether or not I would "Patch up" in the future the leader, B, for some reason took to me and wanted me to be looked after. So that was that. And because the crypts were friendly with the "C-dubs" I had around twenty new friends. Namely Walter, John B, Keith, Todd, Joker and so many more that these days, although I can see their faces, I can't quite recall even singular syllables of their names due to all that has happened. Back in the four-man, in one of two intake cells in the block Todd paced. It was different now. He was already going to look after me, but he had heard about the scribe from B. Todd was in the family. He was happy I had so much support from the family. There were a couple rules to being under them. If someone wanted to "work" I could not turn down the battle. Under no circumstances could I ever be known to be gay. I had to always be honest with the family and I could never steal from the family. Another thing, If I joined anyone, I was not to join the Aryan brotherhood, ADAs, Nazis or any other constituent of the "Hitler lovers." So stipulated.

Dear Dad, Hey Dad. Sorry, I rode out Thursday. I tried a couple times to call but I guess your phone was off. My phone account hasn't been transferred but when it does I will call. I miss you. I don't know how I feel about here yet. 30 day minimum until we can get our first visit and I think they are only 2 hours. If you can, maybe subscribe me to the wall street journal? I miss it. Love, Pat.

Dear Dad, try not to shed too much hair in my helmet. :) Two visits each person/month and they are 2 hours each. Since you are asking I will be completely honest. ABs approached me for the first time, like I knew they would. I kind of knew what they were doing and brushed them off. I met this guy at med bay that was pretty cool. He was the leader of another gang. They aren't trying to get me to join but they are watching after me and now I have like 20 new friends. I have to go to chow but I love you and miss you. Love, Pat.

Dear Dad, Getting weird feelings about the ABs. Will stay in touch. Always love, Pat.

Dear Dad, turns out the victim's family are affiliated with the ABs. The guy I talked to seems to want trouble. I'll keep my head down. Love, Pat.

Dear Dad, Diplomacy failed. Still can't call. And to answer your question, yes. Love, Pat.

I had lived in 3B for several days when I sent these messages. A man short and stocky approached me and began to ask directly about my case. Once he found out my name he seemed to not be interested in who actually committed the crime, only the verdict and my name. He was an AB and after several more days of paranoia I felt like I needed to tell my new found friends; Todd, White and the new guy in the four man cell, Link.

Fight

Darkness lingered in the four man cell. Outside our door the CO could be heard rummaging through our mail at his desk. Outside the window the sounds of the inmates could be heard yelling, throwing trash and loudly playing their music. Once in a while silence would fall like resounding veil thrown into the night - in those moments of solace I could hear a cricket, a cat in the distance, and if I strained I could almost hear the passing of a car far off into the night. I slipped down off my rack and sat on the plastic chair next to the door.

"Todd?" I asked, piercing the darkness. He sat up. "I have a strange feeling about the purebloods."

"Why?" His voice was stifling his confusion with anxiety. I went on to explain everything that had recently happened. When I had finished I admitted that I felt vacuous for even mentioning it. "No" he responded. "You did the right thing." He paused, looking toward Link, then back at me. "I just wish you would have told me sooner. Tomorrow we are going to talk to John B."

I frowned, "For what?".

He shook his head. "This could be more serious than you think." The night dragged on in fitted bursts of sleep. I imagined seven or eight Nazis jumping me then fell asleep again then woke up angry that I was in the situation in the first place, then fall back to sleep. Link shook me awake when the doors finally opened in the morning. I stepped down onto the floor. The cold November morning air blew through the cell making the hair on my arms and bare legs stand on end. One leg at a time I worked my way into the state blue pants, then I put on my state blue shirt and shoes. I looked outside, the air blowing in was enough to convince me that I needed to wear my hoodie and coat. I put each on and walked toward the door.

"Wait!" Todd stopped me. "For now, make sure you stay near either me or Link until we get this figured out. You shouldn't wander off and you definitely don't have a reason to talk to anyone outside the family."

I looked out of the cell, into the dayroom, then back to Todd and nodded. "Yeah, man. That's cool." Link led the way out and I followed. The tension in that dayroom could have been cut with a knife. The family and friends of the family stood out to me. They were all kind, strong individuals who would walk into a war zone if one of the family needed it. The brothers and friends of the brothers stood out to me as money hungry bigots who were well known to turn on their own or go seven or more on one to prove the point that their skinhead insolent brothers would not be beaten, certainly not in a fair fight.

I sent a message to my dad about that time. I told him that the family were the only ones seemingly on my side. They hardly knew me, but I was with them and that was that. It didn't matter that I was white and most of them were black. In my personal prison experience there has been significantly little distinction between races. Occasionally I would find myself disgusted at the behavior of a black man and feel myself slipping into a prejudiced mindset, then I noticed a white man acting the same having the same behavior, and realize that ignorant people are of all races.

At Breakfast and dayroom I realized that I didn't talk to anyone outside the family, anyways. Each and every person that was friendly with me or otherwise not abrasive was affiliated as a blood, crypt, or CWB. Rec was early in the morning, just after breakfast. I walked through my new dilapidated home across the yard with my block to the recreation building. John B. was waiting for me in the basketball court sitting on the bleachers. He waved me over motioning for me to sit with him. When I walked up I noticed that he had one of his closest standing nearby. Not for protection, he explained, but to make sure that nobody is eavesdropping. He asked me to describe to him everything that had happened. I did. When I finished he showed the same concern, but with a reasonably higher degree of sensibility.

"How much time do you have left?", he asked.

"Twenty four with an elbow."

He nodded. "Todd told me that you are trustworthy, are you?" I told him that I was. "What are you here for?"

"Agg burglary, Agg Robbery, Murder and a Gun Spec."

He nodded. "Still have your paperwork?"

"I do."

"Good, people will ask to see it later in your bit. So, tell me what happened." I told him the same story I had been telling for over a year, about my codefendants, the prosecutor and my appeal. "We need to be 100% with each other."

"I know" I told him, confused.

He looked at me for a long moment, then nodded. "Okay, so what's going on is that obviously this guy doesn't like you. He wants you gone and if we don't deal with it soon he will probably take it to the brothers and they'll try to jump you. We aren't going to let them jump you, but we also aren't going to start a war over you. Now, what we are going to do is set it so that you are going to shoot with the one with him. Just you and him, and we aren't going to let anyone else in the cell. I'll set it up for when the doors pop after count, right before lunch. You cool with that?"

I let out my breath. "That's what needs to be done."

He smiled. "Cool. Good luck man, You'll be fine."

I walked back to the block with John and his shadow West. We talked about our cases and doing time. West had a case like mine and had been in prison since he was 15. He knew what my situation was like and gave me good advice. Back in the cell Link and Todd made punching mitts and had me practice.

"One, two, duck: One, two, duck. One, two, duck. One, two, one two, duck."

"I'm telling you guys I already know how to fight." I lied.

"That's okay." Said Link. "But I bet you've never fought in a cell, in prison, have you?"

I stopped.

"That's what I thought." Link's hands had two homemade pads on them and he was running me through my footwork and dodging in the cell. Every time I looked down at my feet he hit me in the head and kept it moving.

"One, two, duck. One, two, duck. One two, one two, duck." Occasionally he would charge me, prompting me to push his head down and to the side. We had forty five minutes before the fight. To them just my first prison fight. To me my first fight, period. But they didn't need to know that. "One, two, duck. One, two, duck. One, two, duck, duck." The longer we worked, the smoother it got. After twenty minutes he stopped. "Alright, we should stop."

"Why?"

He took off the mitts. "It doesn't help you if you are just tired and can't fight when it's time." I realized that it was real. I had wrestled in high school and seen fights here and there, but never fought like I was about to. I sat on my rack and considered where I was. Ten minutes before the doors were going to pop, two cells down the cellie of the guy who I was going to fight yelled out the window for Todd. Todd went to the window and argued for several minutes. He stepped away and looked at Link then to me.

"I have some news. It's not necessarily bad, but it changes things. The brothers know how much time you have and are going to put one of their own at the door and one in here. They want to make sure that you don't try to lock him or stick him." I shook my head and hopped down from the top rack.

"That's crazy. I'm not going to hit him with a sock lock or stab him, we're just shooting the ones."

"He doesn't think that, they figure you have a lot of time and are going to try and prove something."

"That's crazy, why would I-" The doors unlocked.

"We don't have time to argue about this. Listen, just do what we told you and you'll be fine." The three of them left the room. I took my shirt off and threw it on my bed with just enough time to see the brothers' lookout come in followed by the short, stocky guy I was set to fight. Almost immediately time slowed to 200 fps from 24. He stood about four inches shorter than me and made up for the height difference by coming in aggressive. He ducked his head back, down, then threw his first punch. I blocked it with my left arm and his second connected with the right side of my face. I grabbed his hand before it pulled away, and connected three quick jabs with my left hand. He yanked his hand from mine, staggering me, and landed one hard right on my temple. I shook back and tried to remember what I had been taught before coming to prison or what Link taught me, but everything was gone. It was all replaced with me stuck between the desk and bed, backed against the window trading punches with a man who had been preparing to fight every day for years. Each time I connected two jabs he countered with one hard slam straight into my head, slowing the world down even more. The punches didn't hurt, and they were getting weaker, he was getting weaker. I tried to do what Link told me. One, two, duck. One, two, duck. One, two, slam. My vision blurred briefly, then I remembered he was a brother. I saw myself slam him back with my foot, punch him in the throat, follow him to the ground and make him regret coming to my cell. But then I saw his friend stepping in, kicking my teeth out, Todd coming in, more brothers more CWBs, more brothers, more of the family, Nazis, Bloods, more more more. Brothers don't lose, and this would follow me. The point was that I did what most don't, I fought. I went toe to toe. I didn't run, I didn't pay for protection, I did what I needed to. I hit him with a hard right, two lefts and dropped my hands. He hit me with a body shot, body shot, face, face, face.

"Alright, alright." He hit me with two hard bodies and two brothers walked out. I stretched up and moved to the mirror. My face had begun to swell on the left side. Todd came in.
"You did fine, bro, stay back from chow and eat some soups."

"Alright." He walked out, leaving me in the silence. FWOMP, FWOMP. My head throbbed with the blood pouring into the pocket created during the fight. As time went on it began to throb with more and more pain. I put two Ramen soups, crushed up, into a cup and filled it with water from the tap. Once the block had come back from chow, one by one each family member came up to say good job and ask how I was. Once the soups were cooked I got a spoon and tried to eat but my jaw wouldn't open. It would move a half inch down and.. PANG... through my head. I set the cup on the bed and tried to open it. Each time pangs ceased any effort I could muster. Finally I put hands on both sides of my face, pressing into the joints, and opened my mouth with a loud "click!" and an excruciating pang. For the rest of the day and a half of the next I stayed in the cell. Once I came out it was for rec. The swelling had gone down considerably, though it had been replaced by a dark black eye. Todd told me that if anyone asked where it came from to say that I was elbowed while playing basketball. John B. was sitting on the bleachers exactly where I saw him the day before. I shook hands with him and we sat down.

"Nice shiner, Todd told me how it went. I'm proud of how you did, You showed a lot of heart."

I shrugged. "I did what I needed."

He beamed at me for a second. "Have you considered probating? We trust you and you us, I hope."

I nodded. "I do. I'm interested, but I really don't know." While he talked I looked at his forearm and two AK-47s and the Cincinnati "C" on his arm.

"We aren't like these other gangs running around. We are a family, you can see that. If one of our own needs something, they get it. If one of our own is fighting, we fight. Your situation was different because of the repercussions, you understand, anyways we are all in. I want you to patch, I do. But I'm not going to lie, I would rather you not do it if you aren't going to give 100% at all times."

"I understand. I like the connection and dedication within the family. But the only thing that stops me is that with my appeal in I really need to stay under the radar. So, an STG file would really not help." He understood. From that day on, at least to the family, I had proven my worth. I was on their radars. Looking back I can't help but wonder what would have happened if I hadn't been under their wings through that time.

Little San Francisco

"Top range, day room!" The doors popped open all at once with a loud click. Todd walked out of the door followed by me, Link and then White. White walked straight to the pure breeds and disappeared in a crowd of bald ruffians. Todd, Link and I walked down the stairs keeping an eye on everyone around us, always ready to defend or strike, if needed. Link split off at the bottom of the stairs to talk to Carr. Todd walked to John's cell and indicated for me to stay close. I sat at the metal-mesh-table near the closest phone tower, near a group of friendlies. I got in line for a phone and waited. Watching a football game between two Midwestern teams. After several minutes it was my turn on the phone and I dialed my Mom's number. She answered, eating dinner, and put me on speaker so I could talk to her and my Dad. Before the first five minute notification the correction officer walked to me and asked my name.

"McGail." I replied. He pointed up to my cell and told me to pack up, I was going to "2-D." I frowned. "Can I finish my call?" I asked, perplexed.

"No. You're leaving now." I told my parents I needed to go and would call them after I moved. They nervously said goodbye. After climbing the narrow stairs to the top range Todd looked up at me, curious. I entered the cell and started to pack all my belongings in my mesh laundry bag.

"Where you going?" I turned to see Todd in the door.

"2-D" I replied. "They just told me. Write down your info for me. You still have mine, right? He nodded, looking for a pen. "Good. I'll get Links and John's too." I threw my mesh bag on my mat and walked the whole thing down the stairs. At the bottom I was greeted by Keith and Link who also asked where I was going. Keith wished me luck and Link went to go write his information down for me. In the foyer of the block sat a yellow cart made specifically for inmate movements. I sat my mat and mesh bag inside and went back to collect and distribute information. John, through the door, told me he would send a scribe down to the block in the morning. I slid a slip with my information under the door and he slid his to me. Saying a final goodbye to John, Todd, White was nowhere to be found, Link Joker, Walter and everyone else I walked out the door to meet whatever was next for me. The yellow cart barely fit through the door. With some pushing, pulling, paint scraping I got the cart through the door.

Rain was lightly misting the artificially lit night. The monstrous lanterns burning the night were hazy through the rain. On the road to my new home I didn't see a single soul. I walked slowly intentionally to prolong the brisk night air walk. I passed by 3A and could see my new block ahead of me already. I wondered how much different my new block would be. I paused before walking down the road toward my new bock and looked around. Nobody was on the yard, I couldn't even see a CO. I leaned against the cart and sat for a moment and looked up at the sky. A small group of birds passed over me and I thought to myself about how I am so separate and yet so close to the nature that I loved. The dysteleology was ubiquitous to my situation as far as I could see. Everyone moved around meaninglessly and acted meaninglessly until they left after work or after their sentence. I turned down the road to the block and entered the foyer. Leaving the cart half exposed to the outside, knowing I had to take it back, I picked up my mat and walked through the dayroom to my new cell; the bottom range four man in block 2-D. Without looking toward anyone I dropped my mat on the cell's only available rack and walked back out into the rain. After dropping off the cart I walked even slower to the block as there was no need to rush the inevitable. Perhaps the atmosphere in the block would be more relaxed. The first thing I noticed in the block was a girl with long blond hair with her back to me talking to the correction officers at the front desk. When I walked past her I noticed that it wasn't a girl at all but a man with long hair and eyeliner. To the untrained eye, such as mine, from the back or front he almost passed as a female. A phone was open and I beelined for it. In three rings my Mom answered. I told her the new block seemed alright. I didn't think that it would be as bad, there was one, what two, God, three girl looking guys. It would certainly be an interesting stay, that was for sure. The rest of the phone call passed in a blur. Before I knew it we were saying goodbye and I was hanging up. I walked to the four man to move myself in. Just as I was leaving a cave-man walked out the door to get a broom. I excused myself and slid inside. Once inside the cell I glanced around briefly. The cell was certainly cleaner than the last one. I took out nearly all my clothes, letters and files and put them on the tray-style rack, under my mat. Once finished I placed my laundry bag filled with commissary in the corner.

"You don't have a box?" I turned to talk to the caveman who was now holding a broom.

"No." I answered. He slid a metal lock box from under the bunk bed I shared with him, supposedly.

"You can use mine, I hardly use it." After sensing my hesitation he nodded

"I'm not on anything funny, I don't steal. I just don't use it." Still hesitant but slightly reassured I put my commissary and Bible into the box. He introduced himself. His name was Todd, he said I might as well stay locked down because the dayroom would close in only a few minutes. I said okay and continued to unpack and settle. When dayroom closed for the night I was finishing the world news section of the Journal. Hearing the door close I folded my newspaper neatly and laid it under the foot of my mat. My three cellies Randy, E and Todd were fairly relaxed. Randy seemed rather slow and worked in the chow hall every day in the morning from five to noon. He was charged with bank robbery and was surprisingly intelligent, considering. Todd was a former marine who had an attempted murder charge for tying a "Chomo" to a tree and leaving him for dead after severely beating him. They asked me about myself and I ended up detailing the same account I had gave since the first day I was charged. If they held any disbelief, it was dashed when I received the wall street journal that night, which earned me the local nickname "Wall Street."

The next morning was as typical as any other day. We were let out of our cells, just bottom range, early for dayroom. Before the top range was let out for breakfast I was beckoned over to a group of mysterious guys holding the wall in place. They asked typical questions anyone would ask, then let me know "their" block was dangerous. For a low fee I could live comfortable. I told them that I could take care of myself, just as I had since I got into the camp, and that their block was softer than the one I had come from. They brushed me off and I went off to the chow. The day passed by, as did the next week. Without hearing anything from who I learned to be the bloods I assumed I was in the clear. In the dayroom there is a TV placed high on a stone pillar with benches positioned for those who wished to watch it. Watching a football game between two teams I had only then heard of I noticed a short, sickening smile sit down next to me. He nudged me and handed me a piece of paper. I glanced at it and handed it back noticing it was an infamous store list.

"What am I supposed to do with that?"

His smirk grew impossibly larger. "Pick that stuff up, if you don't want any problems."

"I can take care of myself." I felt my blood rushing to my face and my adrenaline empowering me. Dayroom in 2-D is open for the top range in the morning and bottom range at night. The next day it is opposite. Being night time with dayroom closed I locked down. Generally in the four man the light switch stays in the "on" position until roughly midnight. When dayroom locked down at nine I would be left with enough time to read my paper cover to cover and take down general stock prices before mail would come at eleven and we turned the lights out at twelve. Each morning if we didn't have dayroom I would read from one of my books and ease into the day. Once dayroom time would come I would travel the dayroom from the phone to the JPay kiosk to answer any email and then settle any business. Since I was living under the tyranny of a gang I made that as my first priority to deal with, diplomatically. Over the course of a few days I got to know the feel of the apparent leader, Rio. I sat down with him after diplomacy with his Cheshire friend failed and explained to him, using the language I summoned, that with my time and level of funds there was simply no way I would be feeding anyone but me and if I needed to fight his friend and every one of his friends I would. But, I would prefer not to. I had just gotten out of three house and if there was going to be a reason I went back, I would make it worth it. Plain and simple. The next day the Cheshire smile explained the misunderstanding and felt no need for anything rash.

Living in one of the two four man cells in a standard block, as opposed to a two man cell like the one I am in now, has its positives and negatives. A negative was that it is switched out so often that you never know who you'll get. But a positive is that you meet nearly everyone coming into the block so you build a diverse friend group. When Randy moved out, Steve moved in. Steve was extraordinarily intelligent and really good at hiding it. We talked stocks and ethical limitations, him supporting the position of violence to procure monetary gain. The longer I was in the four man the less attached I grew to the newcomers. E left and a white tattoo artist moved in. Todd moved out and a guy with a TV moved in. Steve moved out and a big guy from CRC moved in. To each new guy I was just the long timer in the cell. Two days turned into a month faster than any time I had ever experienced in my life. Just like CRC and County once I got into a routine time flew by me. I transitioned into reading my newspaper in the morning just after chow when we had afternoon dayroom and just after dinner when we had morning dayroom. Meals were the most routine as anything in my life. The kitchen service was contracted to a company called Aramark. They worked on a three week rotation so after a month or two at the camp nearly everybody had a schedule of the meals in their cells. I was no exception.

Toward the end of my time in the four man cell I asked my Mom to start sending me flashcards in French. By the end of the month I would have a dictionary and French poetry book. I began to skip the bulk of my dayroom time to study how to purchase a ticket, greet, inquire formally and informally on how someone is doing and identifying body parts.

The showers were in the dayroom between cells on the first and second ranges. Looking out over the dayroom the showers had curtains and were luxuriously single man. After taking a shower one day, while waiting on the phone, I sat down at the metal-mesh table closest to the tower I wished to visit. Almost immediately I was taken into a conversation by a bald, 20s man with glasses and a beard debating the validity of theological arguments. I took myself out of line for the phone and talked for nearly an hour to the three people sitting with me. Maxie, a bearded intellectual was a white, well versed Muslim in the physical sciences. Reuben was rather quiet, save for sudden absurd outbursts he would share with Maxie; resembling bulls knocking over everything on the table or wrapping their arms around their heads and shadow boxing while tied up in themselves. Stanton was quite, obviously gay, and although very intelligent, made frequent sexual jokes. When it was time to lock down I was confronted by E who told me that everyone at that table had been gay and I should be careful who I am seen talking to. I told him that I wasn't gay and wasn't sure outside of high school why it would matter who I hung out with. Slowly over time I began to embrace my new friends as the closest I had in the block.

One day while I was making a call outside of my dayroom time I was given an "out of place" and "refusing a direct order" ticket. The penalty was ten days on cell isolation; no phone, no JPay. *[No way!]* I quickly learned from Todd that if I took a mirror from commissary like the ones he always had on him, I could open my cell from the outside by sliding the mirror between the door and jam where the lock was located while simultaneously giving a push-pull motion to slide the "key" into place and then pulling the door open. During my time on cell isolation I was out during both dayroom times and would enter/exit my cell at my whim. Looking back, having not keyed a cell in at least four of five months, I think that the appeal was not so much that I could always be out as much as it was my simple rebellion. At WCI, or any prison, where literally every freedom is stripped from you and you are reduced to a number and a sentence, when another freedom is taken away you finally push back. I had never hurt a man woman or child in my life having a sound mind and relatively clear head being pushed and stripped of everything didn't bother me until my rights inside prison were taken. I felt like if I were to make a stand without burning the prison down it would be for calling my mom whenever I wanted to.

In the late hours at a correctional institute you can easily forget where you are. I remember clearly times when we would play spades, hearts, cutthroat, rummy, speed, or even monopoly. In those moments we were not numbers, not sums of the ones before us. We were human. We were real friends who were living though the worst time of our lives, surviving. Through our trials by fire and laughing all the time. And when all was done and they were asleep I would sit. I would watch the cars in the extreme distance, separated more than space could ever describe. I watched the people in all the different cells I could see not surviving, but living. These were not and are not animals in a cage, they are just hurt, misunderstood, sometimes sick people as real and human as you. I would watch the snowfall in those early months of winter knowing the cold and ice was growing near, but thinking my time was almost up.

2 Man (Compadre)

In nearly every block at Warren correctional institution there are two four-man cells for the new inmates and in nearly every block at Warren Correctional Institution a new inmate to the block will first go to one of the four-man cells before being moved to a two-man cell for more permanent housing. At some point when their security is dropped they move to another camp or they may leave the block to move within the compound. When it was my time to move to a two man cell I had very little knowledge of the person I would live with. His name I learned from others around the block was Compadre. He was a "Lifer" who had been in prison since the mid-eighties. From what I understood he was a fairly reasonable man and no doubt easy to live with while I was in the block.

I was given a box leftover from a rideout to store my stuff for the rest of my time at WCI. The box was two feet wide, three feet long and a foot and a half deep. Containing all my clothes, books, sheets, folders, notes, judicial paperwork and state shoes the box was just over half full which I surmise a product of my unscrupulous ability to pack mixed with a healthy attitude regarding the discarding of unnecessary mementoes one would dub as "junk." The cell I was to go to was on the same wall as the four man, directly next to one of the showers. My box and mat were in the new cell in under five minutes from when I was told to move.

I immediately felt a sense of claustrophobia upon entering the new cell. It was twelve feet by six feet with a bunk bed on the right side, a desk, toilet and sink on the left side. The room was kept in reasonable order. There was a TV sitting on the desk and the upper part of the attached cabinet was half full and very neatly divided down the middle Compadre's previous cellie had started a fight in the dayroom right in front of the CO's. This earned him a hole shot and a six month stay in sanctions before being allowed to return to two house, the name for the blocks between lock down and near open dorms. In the end he got what he wanted, which was to change blocks quickly to get rid of his monumental debt in the block. Days later I can remember being hard pressed to find anyone not financially pressed by his leaving. Smart "crash out artists" take large loans of tobacco from tobacco sellers, several days later they go to the store men to payback the tobacco sellers and then use the credit from paying back the tobacco sellers to borrow a lot more food from another store man. Once he had eaten the food and store day had reached him he would hit someone in the dayroom and go to the hole, avoiding the leftover debts from the store men. The difference between store men and tobacco men is simple. A store man buys large quantities of food from commissary and trades it out throughout the month with interest. A tobacco man sells, well, tobacco for food or money in the form of numbers from prepaid "green dots." A tobacco man is very well funded and usually is connected to a gang, while a store man is independent and while he might be able to beat you down in the block, can't touch you outside of it. By paying the tobacco man and "chalking" the store man's debts you run a very low risk of being assaulted and once you get to the hole with 100 dollars of tobacco in your mat you sell the tobacco (which has inflated in price nearly three hundred percent). Once in a new block you can do it all over again. In a year without being caught a crash-out artist can make twelve hundred dollars profit a year, the highest paying job in the camp short of selling heroin.

While I was unpacking, Chewy, a large Mexican man who looked like he should carry a machete, came up to the door. We talked for a few minutes about Compadre and his old cellie. Compadre, said Chewy was "top amigo." It seemed gang related, and I was correct. Later that night when Compadre was in the cell I noticed a full Mexican Mafia back tattoo. He was the genuine article. If I would have had to describe what a high member of the Mexican Mafia was like, it would be him. He frequently paced the cell while I was reading and ranted on and on and on and on and on about how much prison had changed since the beginning. When he first started his bit, he said races held together strong. Now a days, whites are extorting whites. Mexicans, he would say, were the only truly loyal cons left. He set out two or three times to teach me about prison. I learned about everything from how to pinpoint snitches to making poop bombs along with dozens upon dozens of ambiguous rules that not only have I never used I, in fact, can't remember them to save my life.

Poop Bomb

You take a resealable Ziploc style bag that our coffee comes in, poop and pee in it, shake it vigorously, stick the seal end under your target's door and stomp hard.

Life in the cell with Compadre was reasonably sound. We would alternate cleaning when we saw fit and every day I locked down early to watch modern family and ordered delivery food.

In each block there is a society of inmates who make different foods for order and occasionally setup on one of the day room tables as a quasi-buffet. Some make fudge out of peanut butter, stolen sugar and cookies. Some sell taffy made from coffee creamer and orange tang drink or cappuccino. Some sell coffee by the cup. I sold the latter. I bought two eight ounce bags of instant coffee and sold forty cups out of them for twenty five to fifty cent each. I used the profit, usually around ten dollars, to buy grilled cheese sandwiches that my friend Reuben made.

Day and night passed by routinely. Phone calls, read the paper, play rummy until three, chow, dayroom, shower. Oh, I waited restlessly for the shower. Solace. That is the only word that can quantify just what I felt and what I still feel for showers. The shower curtain is plastic, clear at the head and solid throughout the rest. By putting a towel and change of clothes on the curtain rod you effectively isolate yourself. For twenty minutes I was completely alone with the sound of the water drowning out all others. I would stand in the scorching, or freezing water, depending on the time of day, and with my eyes closed picture the day. The inevitable day when justice was done and I could leave this cruel cesspool of violence. After my shower I would go inside the cell, watch modern family and eat two delivered grilled cheese sandwiches. In those times besides my family all that kept me going was knowing that I could take a nice long shower and eat a grilled cheese.

One night Compadre put a piece of metal into his water and plugged it in. Within thirty seconds the water was boiling. When I inquired about the device he explained that it was called a stinger. It was two handles of fingernail clippers sandwiching a piece of plastic and held together by rubber bands. The metal pieces were attached to the power cord and plugged into the wall. When used correctly it could heat water up in almost no time. He laughed to himself. I asked what was funny and he explained that I was starting to look like a hippie. My hair hadn't been cut since CRC and was looking ragged. He asked if I wanted to be put on the barber shop list and I asked what the barber shop list was?.

At Warren Correctional the barber shop is a small outlet between the mail room where you pick up legal mail (also the quartermaster) and the commissary building. Reasonably straightforward. The barber shop is a room with three barber chairs, four waiting chairs on the wall, a full wall mirror typical of barber shops and a desk for the CO to sit at and observe. To get your haircut, even though the inmates are paid by the state to do it, you have to pay them either a yellow bag (three ounces) of coffee, two dollars fifty cents, for a haircut twice a month or a red bag (seven ounces) of coffee, four dollars sixty cent), for a haircut every week. Compadre sent me to his barber and he told me that the first time would be free to make sure I liked his work before "putting him on payroll." I walked to the barbershop and sat first outside, enjoying the frigid air. Then once a seat opened in the shop I walked in and watched the dynamics of the customers and the workers. When it was my turn to get cut I set up in the chair and told him what I liked; a little bit off the top, clean up the sides, shave the neck and ears. I didn't want or ask for a fade and specifically asked not for a fade. An hour and a half later I left the barber shop with a fade, not unreasonably short, and a line up on my hairline indicative of African American descent.

One of the joys I rarely found those days was walking the yard at night. That winter, just a few weeks shy of December, I walked back to the block at night with not a soul around. Looking up at the night sky it is almost possible to believe I was free. I could almost believe that none of this was happening to me and that I was out in the country under the stars again. Alas, before my hummed tune had finished I had reached 2D. The tragedy of that night was that Compadre told me that he was beginning to get irritated with the fact that I spent so much time in the cell. He understood that I was eighteen with life and understandably depressed, but none the less I needed to find a job.

The next day I submitted a request to the chow hall for employment and just a week later I was hired on the spot. The first day I reported to work I walked back into the kitchen and was met with the sounds one would expect to hear at an iron factory. Steam permeated from every surface and was only caught by the stainless steel behemoths that produced nearly fifteen hundred meals, three times a day. My station was in the dish-room, a hovel used for the most obvious task imaginable. I was pointed at the receiving end of a conveyer belt by my "Supervisor" and wished luck. When dishes needed to be washed, pans, cups, trays, baking sheets, mixing bowls, serving equip, etc... they would be brought back to the dish-room. Once deposited the pans were looted of any edible/sellable food, which was then wrapped in Saran wrap and slid down to the mouth of the dish machine. The dish machine had three main sections, each with differently located water sprayers at different temperatures from one sixty five to two hundred degrees and traps to catch the food thrown off the dishes. A dish spends two minutes flat inside the machine from tip to tail. My job was to take the dishes, sort them on a drying rack and put them back into the kitchen or onto the tray racks for reuse. Dish room workers worked the least of any other worker, half days (8 hours) every other day, (typically 32 hour weeks) but worked harder than any other job. The dish alcove is constantly filled with steam reaching two hundred degrees, the floors were always either being sanitized or squeegeed (there was a well justified joke that nothing can go into the dish room without being washed), we cleaned three thousand trays, ninety two pans and countless other dishes each shift from five until just after one. My life started to move in a blur of work, sleep, work, sleep. I only truly marked the days by what newspaper I read. I felt like I was always at work and my rest days fleeted by with incredible swiftness. I would don my white kitchen clothes and walk through the snow to the chow hall. Each day when I walked back to the block from work my clothes would be soaked on the front, and my hands would be pruned and beat red from grabbing the hot pans all day long. I was paid twenty four dollars a month.

The longer I stayed in 2-D the closer I got to my friend Reuben. We began to hang out every day all day I wasn't at work. He was six foot four, two inches taller than me and weighing over a hundred pounds more. While being the nicest and coolest person I ever met in WCI he had a way of being violent when he had to. He was at Lebanon, WCIs big sister institution for several years and learned very quickly to hit first and ask later. By the time I met him, though, he was more than peaceful purely due to the lack of significant violence at WCI. Nearly every day I would sit with him and play rummy. After a couple months he stopped playing and refused to play "that stupid game" ever again. He was in school working on getting his GED and he dreamed of what he could do once he got out of prison. The longer I hung out with him the closer we became until eventually all of my other friends were ancillary and we were best friends. I recounted the travels I had with my family and he told me all of the ways to make money in prison. I told him about my passive shy nature when I was out and he told me about some of his best fights on the street. It had been years since I knew friendship like I knew with Reuben. My closest friends before I caught my case were negative and frequently would scold me if I talked while we were hanging out. I suppose that I left true friends for them because I fantasized about being accepted in the high school I attended though I didn't know that promise was a casuistry for a solution to the most common quagmire. But now I understood. Now I understood that friends are supportive and enjoy having you around and aren't ashamed of who you are or what you say.

While I was Compadre's cellie I began receiving and reading many more screenplays, as well. Among them were *Annie Hall*, *The Grand Budapest* Hotel, *Royal Tenenbaums*, *Pulp Fiction* and *Joe Versus the Volcano*. When I read the screenplays of movies I loved so dearly I felt like I was watching them again. They were my escape from the prison. Henri Chattier escaped by stealth, I escaped by words. I mused the idea of real escape in my mind and eventually resolved to wait on my appeal at the very least to see if the judicial system would finally come through. All I had to do was wait. When my lawyer visited he would repeat the words over and over and over again. Good chance, wait, excited. He was shocked to find out that I had been locked-up five months already. I told him that I wasn't surprised. One hundred and thirty two eternities had passed by me slower than the entire rest of my life had. Every day I was waiting for the day my innocence would finally be known and I could go home. Every day I became angrier and more resolved to stay mentally strong so that whatever I was going to do would happen without unnecessary complications. I had very down days where the whole world was a dark, black abyss and I had days where everything was right and not any amount of fence could hold my spirit. I prayed too. Though I didn't pray quite as frequently as I did at CRC I thought it important that I talk to God. I would always feel a sense of peace after in a way that the solace of a shower couldn't quite satisfy. The appeal was not, however, a topic of conversation that I usually enlisted. The talk of innocence was a contrived man's talk. It was a form of speech whose quality was for not in the company of inmates. Reuben was the only one who knew we were working on it and that I was innocent. I told him about how I had visited Spain and Russia. I told him about trouncing in Prague and being forbidden from Amsterdam. I confided that the tattoo on my arm wasn't from acid, it was the product of myself and an extraordinarily strange brother sketching in a spontaneous way. I told him about my family and hopes for the future and he hold me his. Sometimes the best friends you ever have are met when you are at the bottom.

Christmas Eve

Every time I have had a visit in prison I always felt like a child on Christmas morning. From the time I left a visit to the time I walk into the next I counted down. Three weeks, one day, twenty-two days, sixty six meals, eighteen newspapers, three breakfast cakes, five hundred twenty six hours. Twenty five. Twenty four. When my name was finally called by the CO my heart skipped a beat. With labored breath I walked to the visiting room past all the other blocks on my road. Each visit brought with it new weather. The sun was shining, the cold wind bit me, the rain fell torrentially on the late fall forgotten leaves. Through all conditions I had one objective: the visitation building.

When you first walk in you are isolated in a foyer area. You can see the visiting room through a locked glass door but have to wait until a CO is available to check you for weapons. I stood there with the sun falling off of me. I stood with rain dripping, I stood with bones thawing, waiting through the longest minutes of my life. One by one more and more inmates filed in. Two, three, four. Regardless of how many of us were in the room, silence was always upheld. We all understood how important those seven thousand two hundred seconds were. It was not a lousy phone call for a quarter hour in a loud block. It wasn't the white crisp paper shoved under our doors every night from Aunt somebody and brother whoever. It was a hundred and twenty uninterrupted minutes with mom, dad, son, daughter, sister, brother. To us and to them it was the most important two hours of the day. To most of us, it was also the moments we lived for. Every day of my life at WCI was about seeing my family again. Just to hear their voices was a light in the dark. When everything, **everything** in my world felt like it was crashing down it made a paramount of difference to be able to pick up the phone and hear their voices. Just to know that somebody, anybody, still believed in me was what kept me going. It kept me alive knowing that I needed to live for them too. With innocence and family on my side I made it through the absolute darkest time of my life. When the clock struck the hour it was time. The only thing standing between me and my families embrace was a quick search of the most pertinent areas.

After being called into the small room used for the searches I was confronted with a cage to search inmates from seg and a podium. Near the cage for the CO to stand, hooks on the walls for our coats and jackets (which were not permitted in the visitation room) and plenty of open floor space for the actual searches. Two at a time we were called in. By December, four months into my odyssey, I knew exactly what to do without any instruction or direction. When the inmate walks into the strip room he is to present his identification card and visitation pass to the correctional officer on duty. He is then to hang up any jackets or coats as they are not to be worn in the visitation room. The inmate is then to remove all clothes that are then to be inspected. The inmate will show the under sides of his feet, squat and cough. When permitted to enter I donned my clothes faster than when I was caught in my girlfriend's bed by her dad. On normal days I was stripped, searched, dressed, and in the visitation room before the other was even undressed. Two hours. One twelfth of a day, one eighty fourth of a week, one three hundred and thirty sixth of a month, then it's gone. The walk back to the block was always the hardest part. I would walk slowly with my head turned in a chance to see them walk away. If by chance I caught their gaze I would raise an arm in silent farewell and carry myself back to the block. Two weeks on the nose until the next visit. No- they would vacation for Christmas. One day under three weeks. Twenty days, sixty meals, seventeen newspapers, one million seven hundred and twenty eight thousand seconds, one million seven hundred and twenty seven thousand nine hundred and ninety nine, ninety eight, ninety seven... The road walking back to the block was rarely in use and I walked slowly, counting and calculating, ninety four, ninety three, ninety two.

For most of the winter, especially Christmas, I only did two things that I cared about - well, three. I read the newspaper every day, I talked to my family on the phone, and worked in the chow hall. I couldn't write, I didn't work out, I hardly went to the commissary except for food, and I certainly didn't gamble. Work was hard but it kept me from the truth of where I was. In the steam filled factory I would drift off into my own world. In the very beginning of working there every day was a challenge. There was a certain flow to the work place I simply didn't fit into. The current was very aggressive and seemingly erratic. Often I couldn't find where to put a pan or a tray of a specific size and had to wade through the army of cooks, bakers and porters to find the hidden niche where the dish belonged. After a couple weeks not only did I understand the rhythmic jig, I embraced the chaotic flow of the space. I noticed that the places for the dishes were both definite and arbitrary. Employees were fired and hired so fast that the locations of various dishes were although generally the same always slightly different. Early on I made the mistake of trying to follow a set of workplace rules that weren't even there. I found that the best way to work at the kitchen was to be assertive, a skill I fear that was not so easy to acquire. Rather than travel with the current I made my own current. I embraced the chaos around me and made people move for me, not vice versa. I chose where the dishes went and soon the people I worked with assimilated.

The nights were my favorite time to work. When the floors were sanitized and the machines cleaned I was finally allowed to leave. The cold air nipped at my face, letting me know that Christmas was on its way. A light sheet of snow was falling from the sky and through the falling snow I could just make out the lights of Lebanon Correctional on the hill. My blue and grey hell had a few beauties. Walking alone down the road to my block with the crunch, crunch, crunch of snow under my feet was certainly one. The closer I came to the block the slower I walked, dreading the inevitable. All too soon I dove into the sea of decibels. **The inmate is to sign in and out upon entering and leaving the block.** My shower bag, already prepared, was waiting for me. After quickly showering and putting on fresh clothes I slipped into my empty cell. Compadre was a porter and so I rarely didn't have the cell to myself. I slipped his stinger into water and turned on the television for modern family. When my water was boiling I unplugged the stringer and lifted it from the water. I admired the ingenuity required to craft such a clever device. The cord was slightly stripped and clearly well worn. I sat down in our plastic chair with tea steeping, watching the shows that rewarded my successful day. Eight thirty meant a half hour until lockdown. I turned off the television and climbed into my top rack. For the remaining half hour with headphones donned I practiced French flashcards. C'est dommage. Quotidiennement. C'est tout bien, M'erre. Je t'aime, moi copine.
When I heard a Pepsi crack I knew it was television time again. I tucked my flash cards under my mattress and watched the droll entertainment. When I heard Compadre's soft snoring I turned off the set and lay staring

at the ceiling with Fleet Foxes, James Blake, Trampled by Turtles or NPR gently humming in my ear. I suspected that my appeal would be filed in February. Generally it would take five months from then to hear an opinion on the matter. From there two days or so and I would be released. Two months to February, seven months to opinion, two days to leave. Today was the twenty third of December. Eight plus thirty one, plus twenty eight plus thirty one plus thirty plus thirty one plus thirty plus probably fifteen plus two. Two hundred and six days. Six hundred and eighteen meals left. Four thousand nine hundred and forty six hours, forty five minutes remaining. The morning would be lightly raining - a protest that the underworld couldn't hold me. I would be wearing light brown corduroy pants, black underwear (boxer briefs), black socks with red and blue stripes, white V-neck undershirt, cornflower blue dress shirt, brown dress shoes, blue stripe tie, tortoise shell glasses. Within five minutes of being outside the gate freedom would hit me. Twenty four years to life in prison would mean my life. I would immediately understand that my life was entirely back in my hands. The world would be mine to explore.

Just before Christmas I was called to the investigator's office. In the days before I had been making house plans on butcher paper to pass the time. At one point the CO had demanded to see them, thinking that they were of the prison. Walking down to the investigator's office I could only think that this had something to do with it. The investigator is in the same building as the visiting room. When I walked into the foyer the glass door stood ajar. Following the hallway the investigator was at the very end. I knocked and was told to wait in the waiting area just outside the office. I sat down and while nervously groping in my pocket I found a tea bag. Not having a cup I decided that it was just as good to sit it in my mouth like a pouch of dip. Within seconds my mouth was completely dry. I walked back down the hallway trying each door until I came to an unlocked bathroom. I turned on the faucet and took a drink of water from my hands. When I closed the bathroom door on my way out a voice echoed through the hall.

"What are you doing?" It was the investigator.

"I was just getting a drink of water.? He frowned.
"What's in your mouth?"

"Uh, tea bag - Ahh a tea bag." I pulled it from my mouth and threw it away. His eyes narrowed.

"There's someone here to see you." He motioned to a door on his right. I walked to the door and entered. A tall, balding man followed from the investigator's office into the small "Interrogation" style room. His name was Detective Sloan. My face tightened. Sitting across from me, just two feet in front of me was the man who knowingly helped convict me of a crime he knew I didn't participate in. Within choking distance was one of the characters of my worst nightmares.

He smiled and let me know that he was sorry he had to come so close to the holidays. I'm sure he was. He said he **{knew}** that I perjured myself at trial.

"I didn't lie." He stopped me. He said he knew that my lawyer had made up the story I told at trial. Unlikely, I thought, I told him what happened mere days after it happened. He wanted to only prosecute those responsible and could protect me if I testified against my attorney. I kept silent and gritted my teeth as the devils silver tongue glistened in the mid-morning light. When he was finished talking I asked if he was done. He was. I stood up and left the room. I fumed all the way back to my block. The nerve of those people. I thought to myself. Their audacious dishonesty was simply amazing. Back in the block I dialed the number into the phone to reach my mom, 1-1-7-0-9-8-7-1-5-5-5-5-#-5-5-5-7-0-7-8-#. She answered in three rings. I always loved being as furious as my mom about something. Our anger was comparable and when combined we would destroy anything in our path. When the call ended I just stared into my cell.

Christmas was anything but merry. I wouldn't say that is was dismal, but the day was almost identical to any other. For lunch we had some Thanksgiving style meal and received a sack dinner. Back at the block most Christmas greetings were met with hostility. Once you start doing a large amount of time most people disregard holidays. Christmas, Thanksgiving, birthdays, they were all just one more "X" on the calendar. Just one day closer to the outdate or parole hearing. Acknowledging holidays is acknowledging that the day is different than any other day. Then they would have to take time to get back into a routine. For nickel, dime, quarter and lifers the most important thing is to keep moving. The first couple years go slow, the middle years go fast and the last years go slow. They also never associate with short timers. I would be a long timer, "Quarter with an elbow" or twenty five [four] years (quarters) to life (elbow, coming from "L" for life). Short timers to me would be anyone with less than ten years left. Nobody doing twenty years wants to talk to anyone doing twenty months. By the time you get close, they leave. For the last two years all you hear is "only nineteen months left." all the way until they leave. Laying in my rack on Christmas, staring up to the familiar ceiling I couldn't help but wonder how many Christmases I would be staring up into penitentiary ceilings. Just one? Thirty? I supposed only twenty three Christmases left. Those questions I still ask myself, staring up into the just as familiar ceiling. How many more nights must I wake up to the same cell, the same rack, the same injustice? How many days must I count down to the unknown. Is it really only a hundred and seventy eight more meals? Or, is it more like twenty six thousand? The Christmas passed by unnoticed. Another call, another meal, another nap, another episode of modern family, another chapter read, another day. Nine thousand eight hundred eighty minutes, seventy nine, seventy eight.

Reuben (Le Pays)

My box felt bloated when I moved over to Reuben's cell. The cell was just on the other side of the shower I flanked. Once all of my stuff was in the cell I set out to unpack my life into a new cell. The rack and cabinet were on opposite sides of the room than the cell that I was moving from. Reuben's cellie had been moved to the merit block and I was the first he asked to take his place. I had been hanging out with Reuben a lot so it was nearly a no-brainer, though my gut told me that it was a bad idea. Going against my instinct I told him that I would move in. Compadre took it the hardest, personally taking blame for me wanting to move. I explained that it wasn't that I didn't enjoy being his cellie but I thought that Reuben and I had more in common and would be a better fit. I didn't mention that free fudge and grilled cheese sandwiches was a massive benefit as well.

When I ran my hand through my hair it was now just peeking between my fingers and the recent haircut was fading. With my belongings half unpacked I sighed wondering how many more cellies I would have, how many more times I would have to move. To get it off my mind I opened the cell door and walked to the CO's desk.

"Can I have the broom?" He took my ID and gave me a broom. The cell was nearly all ready clean, though sweeping the rest of the dust and dirt out gave me a sense of accomplishment. When I had given back the broom I filled an empty trashcan with water and kitchen disinfectant and scrubbed the floor with my shower rag. On my hands and knees I polished the cement with the industrial cleaner. Once I had dried the floor I sat back on my rack and closed my eyes.

The fog rolled across green fields. The warm sun licked the dew drenched morning. My house stood isolated in the patchwork of dying soy, corn and bean fields. My childhood room was blackened and engulfed, the hallway was thick with smoke and flames creeped down the crown molding. Family memories were tainted with the hot destruction, the carpet bubbling and smoking. My barn was teetering on its burnt supports and inside sat everything I had ever dreamed. It's heart, the hollow frame of the room I was building. Not only an unfinished project but a monument to everything I lost. My life was frozen on October 31st, 2013. Seventeen years old and never free again. I stood, chained to a tree near the field. Watching hopelessly, as my life burnt. I opened my mouth to scream and thick, black smoke billowed from my rotting...

"Pat!" The CO was standing out the door and Reuben stood next to the rack. Count time requires every inmate to show movement to indicate life. I hopped down and sat down into the chair. I didn't tell Reuben about the dream, but asked the question I always dreaded. I never asked the people I knew why they were in prison until I became really close to them. I didn't care why he was here but I hated the thought of him spending the rest of his live in that place. He smiled and brushed it off. He had three years left.

Reuben is still the most interesting person I've met in Prison. He stood at Six-four at just over two hundred pounds. He was twenty two and acted like a sixteen year old. Just about the age he was when he was first locked up. He had a troubled childhood. From bouncing around in custody battles to homelessness to early drug addiction and very early sexualization he was in every way not supposed to be in prison. He had previously been in rehabs and intensive psychiatric care facilities and needed intensive therapy badly. He started his "bit" at Lebanon then came to Warren. At Lebanon he learned that safety was with violence. He would talk for hours about the fights he had been in or how he hadn't talked to his Mom in two years. A fact that is evident to me now. He used a metal hot plate made out of a crock pot as a grill to make grilled cheese sandwiches. He was gay, likely not due to the sexual actions but to the emotional connection. He yearned desperately to be close to someone. Explaining one day to me he had remembered that he liked hugging and holding hands with the people he dated at Lebanon infinitely more than anything else. He forced so many people out of his life, scared that they would leave like his family did, that when he found somebody that stayed he would hold on with everything he had to ensure they wouldn't leave him. He was alone and he was sad. Writing these words for the first time I'm surprised at what I say. He always was a friend who revealed remarkably little to those around him and they had to put it together to understand who he was.

After my fight two weeks before I moved I had a small knot on my temple where a blood vessel had burst and hadn't fully healed. Compadre had convinced me to contact health services so that a doctor could look at it closer. After two weeks I had finally heard back and was to see the doctor. After count cleared I presented my pass to the CO and went to the medical building. When I arrived at the health services building I was instructed to sit and wait until the doctor would be ready for me. While I was sitting I made notice of the comings and goings, the process in the pseudo-clinic, the dynamics between inmate porters and CO's, and dynamics between COs. The CO opened a new can of chewing tobacco, took one "dip", and threw the rest away. Minutes later the inmate took the can to be emptied. The next day that same tobacco would be dried and sold as cigarettes for four dollars apiece. (It should be noted that each cigarette is roughly a fourth of one bought on the street, or a "Cadillac"). The doctor had nothing of consequence to say, the bump was common in blunt force trauma and would subside in a matter of weeks.

When I left I went to my block. Once I arrived I put on my kitchen whites over my blues and headed out the door to work. The roads had turned gray from all the walking traffic on top of the snow. A light snow was falling and by the time I got out of work all the walking traffic would be covered and look fresh and new again. The boiling water in the dish room was scalding to my frosted hands. One by one I counted the trays going past me to practice French. Un, Deux, Trois, Quatre, Cinq, Six, Sept, Huit, Neuf, Dix …Quinze, Dix-neuf, Vingt, stack. Every twenty trays I would stack them onto the cooling racks. There is no clock in the dish room so I based my work day on trays seen. Seven hundred trays was half time, we would be receiving cooking utensils, fourteen hundred meant that everyone had passed through. All that would be left was several hundred segregation trays, serving utensils, clean the dish room, eat lunch, prep the machine for dinner, rinse, and repeat. Once the dish room was cleaned after we ate dinner and the kitchen was shut down I opened the machine, cleaned out the food traps, drained the cells of water, sprayed down the machine, sanitized the machine, refilled the cells, emptied them, replaced the traps, sanitized the floor again and left into the cold dark.

The snow was falling thicker, and I could feel it crunch under my feet. Solace. The wind bit into my soaked clothes, though I walked slow nonetheless. The only moments of my life that could be described as peaceful were the nights I spent walking from the hot hell of work through the icy solace to the warmth of a shower and my rack. It was moments like that that made me realize I could live here for a long time. Prison isn't so bad. The bad part is knowing you can't leave. I paused outside my block for a moment, with my hand on the handle. I took a breath, two, three. And out, two three, four, five, six, seven. The cacophony of sound filled my ears as soon as the door opened. I waved down a CO and got them to open my cell. Reuben had a small laboratory of cooking set up. I stepped in apprehensively.

"What are you about to do?" he asked, stopping.

"Well, I was going to go take a shower."

He seemed to not notice or hear that I spoke. "Want to help me make taffy?"

I sighed. "Sure."

He smiled. "Great!"

Taffy

Taffy, in prison, can be made a multitude of ways. The most popular of which involves taking a bag of nearly pure vitamin-C disguised as "breakfast drink" and mixing it in a bowl with three quarters of a bag of creamer. You put a small amount of water in with it and stir until it is impossible to stir further. Next you put the bowl in the microwave. Watch the bowl closely and once the mixture bubbles to the top take it out and mix vigorously. Place the bowl back into the microwave and wait again for it to rise. Continue this process until the "Grit" is removed from the mix. Once it is, take it back to your cell. Quickly take a trash bag and rip it so you can lay it flat on your locker box. Once it's flat pour the mix in two strips on the box to cool. After twenty or so minutes the mix can be cooled into taffy. Take a knife, ID or new playing card and cut the mix into fourteen equal pieces.

Each piece sells for fifty cents, each batch merits seven dollars, four dollars profit. Once I finished I took my shower bag and jumped in with just five minutes till lockdown. I stood and let the water pour over me, feeling each of the muscles in my back loosen one by one and stress fall onto the shower floor with the dirt grime and sweat. I stepped out and walked the six feet to my cell and locked the door. When I walked in Reuben was standing with a rubber band in one hand and a plastic wrapped up ball in the other.

"What is that?"

He shrugged. "What's what?" I pointed at the ball.

"What's that in your hand?" He looked at his hand and back to me.

"Don't worry about that!"

"But what is it?"

He threw his hands up. "It's nothing! Just drop it!"

I pointed at it. "That's weed isn't it? You're selling weed?"

He turned around. "It's not weed."

I raised my voice. "Then what is it!?"

He equaled my voice. "It's heroin!"

"What!"

He scolded me. "Lower you voice!"

I nearly whispered. "Why the hell are you selling heroin?"

He shook his head "I'm not selling it, I'm holding it for someone else."

"Who?" I asked.

"Why are you so nosey?"

I shrugged, "I don't know. Why are you even holding it? It sure doesn't look like much."

Staying Me

He scoffed. "You obviously haven't seen heroin before." I shrugged. "Look." He unwrapped the small plastic ball and put the whitish ball on the desk. He picked up a razor blade and shaved off a piece the size of the tip of a pen. "See this?"

I nodded. "Yeah, so what?"

He pointed at it. "That's fifty dollars."

"What!!!" He hit my arm.

"Shut up stupid. This is all about six hundred dollars, honestly maybe more."

I shook my head. "That's crazy, how do you hold it?"

He laughed "I take a rubber band and tie it to these." He shook his balls. "Clang!" Something had fallen out of his pants. I pointed.

"What's that!"

He picked up a knife. "Chill, dude. It's a knife." I threw up my hands flabbergasted.

"Oh, that's all! Why do you have a knife?"

He shushed me. "I sell them to the guy that I hold the heroin for." I stood, astonished, then broke my trance and put away my shower stuff. "What?" I shook my head. "What? you're not cool with me holding this stuff?"

"You do you, man. If you want to go to Lucasville over a couple bucks; then.."

"Stupid, first of all, he's paying me more than a couple bucks. Second, don't worry. You won't be implicated."

"How do you know?"

"Because I know. I made some fudge, take a piece." I took a piece and jumped up on my rack to read. After a while he shut off his television and said goodnight. I sat up for a while after his breathing slowed, considering whether or not I should have moved in when he was doing things like that.

Perhaps he was right and I wouldn't be implicated and everything would be fine, or maybe I would be sent to Luke to be stabbed. After all I was here for being accused of something I didn't do. I fell asleep and had fleeting dreams of all the possibilities.

1A

Within days of Christmas I stopped counting down. When it came down to it I had no idea when I would leave, when my appeal would be heard by the courts or even when it would be submitted. I would lay awake arbitrarily counting down weeks , days, meals, hours, bowel movements, seconds, phone calls. Surprisingly, as soon as I stopped surreptitiously counting, the days began to go by faster. Days, weeks would go by without even a thought. My time was still filled with my free time devoted to reading the works of Vladimir Nabokov. My brother's girlfriend, Hannah, sent me his collective works and I had begun to cypher through the dense, matted layers upon layers of literary prowess residing between the bleached whites. December was a blink of an eye after Christmas, we did not stay up to watch the ball drop. January was as fleeting as foxes.

Toward the middle of January my good friend, Pat, left two-delta for the Merit block, one-alpha. There are a couple of ways to get to the merit block. Pat, a short body builder from Jersey requested months in advance to be put on the waiting list. Eventually, he was asked to move up and he accepted. He packed his belongings and was gone the next day which was of no real consequence to me, I worked with him and so I saw him every other day. Shortly thereafter Reuben, who had put in his request at the same time as Pat was asked to also go to the merit block. He declined and after much asking he admitted that he wanted to stay in the cell with me because he wanted to be more than friends. After a long discussion beginning with my sexual preference, looping around to me being closed minded and a short debate about the difference between heterosexual and closed minded and finally an hour of silence he conceded that it wouldn't work and accepted the offer to go to the merit block. I helped him take his belongings to the Merit block. He told me that he would pull what strings he could to get me to merit as soon as possible. Thankful, I shook his hand and wished him the best. That night I sat for several hours in the silence of my now single man cell contemplating who my new cellie was going to be and if/when I would be moved to the merit block. I woke up--to silence. Not the whistle of a commissary crock pot, not the hum of a television or the rustling of life. I woke up to silence. Darkness shrouded the world.

The only force powerful enough to wake me was the ritual of noise at six thirty. The jingle of keys was heard. I stood and waited at the door. The CO saw me in the door and unlocked it. Breakfast. Nearly the entirety of my day was defined by silence. A cell alone after so long with company was impossible to overcome. It was deafening, forbearing, obsolete. The days, every day for months had been defined by a big gay friend named Reuben. Impossible, flirtatious, loquacious and entertaining. Reuben was a large bipolar sack of friendship and now he was gone.

On the second day of my isolation during the morning count a CO popped my door and asked if I had problems with anyone in the block. When I responded negative he told me that I was about to get a new cellie in an emergency move. From across the block I could see his door open. If there was a man I would not have wanted to cell with it was Lefty Al. A 50-year-old black man who had spent most of his life in prison and by all accounts would spend the rest of it as well. He was impossible to live with evident by the fact that he frequently changed cells. He was a known child molester who watched children shows and soap operas all day. I didn't care who I had to cell with, but I wanted to be out of the cell with him. Just one day into living with him he asked why I hadn't gone to the bathroom while he was in the cell. I needed to leave. Two more days later I got my wish. Reuben had certainly pulled strings. Usually, it takes nine months to be eligible for merit. I had been here four months. Usually, you have to be ticket free. I had two tickets for "out of place and disobeying a direct order." Usually, you have to send in a request to be on the waiting list. I just had a friend that paid the sergeant's clerk four dollars. I was called up to the sergeant's office in 1-A on Wednesday. He wanted to be sure that I had no problems with LGBT inmates. I thought it an odd question but still gave my honest answer.

On Thursday I was reassigned from 2-D to 1-A 126. Immediately when I arrived I understood the sergeant's question. Looking down at me was a six-four, three hundred and fifty pound black transgender named Coa Coa. As it turned out, I got to merit so quickly not because Reuben paid off the clerk, but because Coa Coa was under the PREA program as a victim. He had been eligible as a transgender inmate and because he had been classified as a victim of rape, he could choose who he wanted to cell with. When Reuben arrived at merit and saw his friend Coa didn't have a cellie he had Coa request me to the sergeant and that's how I got to the merit block so quickly.

Once I settled myself into the cell I walked out to look around the block. The most significant difference was that our doors were open all day except for an hour in the morning and an hour in the afternoon for count. Instead of metal grate tables in the day room we had wood tables with plastic chairs. The other large benefits to 1A was that the TV room had a small library, direct TV and the dayroom had pull-up bars, dip bars, pushup bars, and exercise bikes. The downside was that I was taken out of my routine. Time instantly slowed to a halt and the events for the next two days dragged into eternity and were magnified ten-fold.

An old school black man was coming back into his cell when he realized that his television had been stolen. Within an hour he was approached by a gang member.

"I got your TV. You can get it back for 100 in commissary." The old man agreed. The next day, my first full day at merit, he was standing in the crowded, twisting line at commissary just ahead of the thief. He bided his time. Waiting. Waiting. Once they reached the center of the line, far from both the door and a CO and sandwiched between fifty people on either side he took a knife from his pocket. When the report of events reached me they had become vivid with the events that followed with sound effects and such. I don't wish to bore the reader with such details and so I will go on to explain what happened that night. Shortly after eleven at night the mail for the day slid under the door. Two manila envelopes with screenplays from my Mom, a newspaper from the Wall Street Journal and a letter. A letter to me. A letter to me from J. H. Who is J H.? I thought for a while just looking at the outside of the envelope then finally opened it.

Four years ago, freshman year of high school I sat two seats behind and one to the left of a beautiful girl. She was smart, mature for her age and a gymnast. She was the popular girl who I always had a crush on and had sent me a letter. Four years later. In Prison. It was funny to me that friends I had since I was four years old couldn't write me but a girl I never talked to and shared a room with for an hour a day for thirty six weeks could write a motivating and encouraging letter out of nowhere, because she cared. It is a curious thing: to see just by being away how many people care and are genuine human beings and how many only care so long as you are right before them. This principle of life is learned by every inmate sent to a correction facility.

Whether you have twenty four years or just four months. A man of the latter that night coped with the incarceration with "strips". He took Suboxone strips, a drug used to treat heroin addiction and generally slipped into the prison by way of mail and certain correction officers that won't be mentioned although any inmate in the institution could spot them. The young man with just four months to go was taking Suboxone with his cellie. The doses were large and potent and the next morning he was found dead on his rack. He overdosed in the night and his cellie never woke up to save him. Sometime between lunch and breakfast the yard was cleared, we were locked down and they brought in an ambulance. The deceased cellie was waiting for his ride with the coroner and the living one was being taken to the hospital. The media never caught wind, we had always been scrutinized to secrecy to such things. Nonetheless that night Norbert, Aka Coa Coa and I watched the news for any word on our departed brother in chains. Eleven o'clock came and once again a letter was slid with my newspaper under the door. This one was from the grandmother of a girlfriend I once had. Although it didn't bear a return address it was kind, sincere and supportive. Around two in the morning Norbert and I grouped around the window to the sound of a four wheel drive gator. It was the clinic emergency medical vehicle. It was driving from the small segregation block to the clinic. The next day we heard that one of the inmates killed himself. In the first week I was in merit two inmates died, one inmate nearly died from an overdose and an inmate almost died in a stabbing. None of it would reach the news. None of it would reach our families save for the hints dropped over the phone, in letters or at visits.

The end of the week brought disappointment. The days leading up to the overdoses Reuben had mentioned in passing doing Suboxone strips and asked me if I wanted any. I refused and he dropped the subject all together after the overdoses. Toward the end of the week I went looking for Reuben only to find him wild-eyed and inebriated. We sat in the day room for an extended time. For a while, maybe an hour, until he finally grew silent, and then pale. He said he didn't feel well and went up to his cell. When I came up later he had thrown up several times and was much paler. He had a radial and femoral pulse which indicated to me that his blood pressure was not low and his pulse was slightly below normal, a symptom I wrote off to laying down and relaxing in a stupor of drugs. Until day room closed at nine fifteen I repeated the same tests in twenty minute intervals to be sure his situation was not deteriorating. I gave him water when he needed water and made sure he stayed laying on his side. Besides the periodic verbal abuse I took care of him with respect and kindness. The verbal assault, I felt, was warranted due to the terrible decision he made shortly after one of our fellow inmates died from the same drug and possibly the same shipment. Oh, I was so happy to be in merit.

I find myself looking with distaste on my attitude towards this situation I wrote about. I do remember that situation because of my nerves during the encounter. I constantly worried that something else could be mixed into the strips and at any moment I could look over and he could have been dead. Though, now typing and Reuben standing up a couple of feet away trying to fix an old radio I should have known everything would be fine. And I'm glad it was.

Brutus

"Everyone out of the dish room!" The CO in charge of the kitchen, Daniels, and one of his cronies, Butch walked in. Daniels hit the shut off switch on the machine, stopping the light rain from the busted water line on the steel beast's top. We all began walking out, Butch stopped me.

"Not you, McGail."

Daniels walked behind the machine. "What's under here, McGail?" I remained silent. "Come on, make this easier. "

I sighed, "Some patties". He pulled two loafs of bread from beneath the machine.

"And bread?"

I shook my head. "No, no bread."

He stood up with the bread. "This was the only thing under there. "

I shook my head again. "No, I didn't put bread under there. Check the camera." The two shared a look and Daniels looked at me.

"Get what you put under there." I walked behind the machine and kneeled in the water next to the mold on the wall.

"There's nothing under here. " I stood up.

Butch glared at me. "Look again." I knelt down and looked under the machine, passing the spot that I had hid the food in the machine.

"Nothing is here."

Butch pointed toward the door. "Get out." I walked out only to be interrupted by a large, dumb looking CO with a nasty grin and the smell of Kamchatka Vodka on his breath.

"Should I cuff him up?"

Daniels' voice came from behind the machine. "No, he's right. There's nothing under here." Butch looked at the brute. Take him to the captain's office. The brute walked me out of the room. Once we were clear of Daniels he put cuffs on me and continued the walk. The air gave a hint that Spring was on its way.

"Nice weather, huh?" He remained silent. "You know, it's strange how the administration tells us not to take food from the chow hall, but then at the end of the night they tell us to throw away tens of pounds of food. " He grunted with a sickening smile. "Well, I just don't know. Especially since they really don't feed us enough. You know, they feed us enough for a normal adult male. Five six, a hundred and sixty pounds. Fully grown. But what about someone like me; Six-two, A hundred seventy supposed to be damn near two hundred. Eighteen, still grow..."

"Shut up."

I scoffed with derision. We walked for a minute or two until we reached the building that contained the captain's office. The building was pleasantly warm. Being one of the only climate controlled buildings on the compound it was always the perfect temperature to keep the mindless drones operating at optimum levels. Just as we walked into the building a flood of lieutenants, sergeants, captains, and all other arbitrary combinations of stripes and bars poured out of one of the doors and laid waste to the ounces of self-respect they had left, yelling profanity and reaching impressively close to my face, no doubt a nod to their collective failed military careers. In their midst was LT. Jordan. He was the quietest of the bunch, but made one point abundantly clear, I was fired.

"What about?"

"No."

"Not even?"

"Done." There was a staff extravaganza when I began to explain. There was feigned derision when I deflated, and they were there just in time to pump me full of fresh insults. I lost, I never even competed. They were the top dogs and the key holders. They were of such high statue they would not be called by anything except their last names. They had thoroughly evolved beyond pleasantries to peon-peers. To us they must, MUST be addressed as nobles. Yes sir, I am worthless. Yes sir you will always have a better life than me. Yes Sir, you just search my cell and give me a hard time because your wife is cheating on you. We were not even allowed names. Inmate. You. I am 709871. You are Sir.

The air was colder. Stale. The walk back to 1A felt as if it would take an eternity. Now it was my turn to ignore the ogre walking with me. Twice he attempted to make insolent remarks. Twice I showed no emotion toward him. Approaching the block while mumbling to myself I happened upon a word synonymous for both cat and correction officer. He raised an eyebrow and looked sideways at me.

"If all COs are pussies, why don't you try something?" I looked around, uncomfortable. "There are no cameras. Don't worry. Do it. Hit me." I pictured all of the vile things I would like to do to him. None of it would matter, of course. He would call the goon squad and as a unit he and his team of steroid injected mace spraying high school rejects would bounce me off the pavement like a basketball and cover every orifice of my body with mace. Then, they would send me to Lucasville where I would be subjected to the ingenious nature of the criminally insane. When men arrive, they get excrement thrown on them. At rec, they get stabbed. In the cell, the one man cell, they get human waste thrown on them. At night inmates yell from across the block. No sleep, human waste and stabbing. For one punch. I stayed silent. "That's what I thought." He blew past his food hole. The rest of the walk he had a fat, ugly John Wayne swagger. How proud he was for beating the eighteen year old, a hundred and sixty pound inmate at a verbal game of chicken. Yes, very impressive. Once we got to my cell he began recounting, loud enough so the other CO's could hear, about how I, in fact, was weak and incompetent and had the nerve to talk down about Correctional officers but I was hardly listening, looking around the cell and up at the ceiling. When at last I couldn't bear the monotony of listening to his grunts I interrupted.

"Why are you upset?" I asked again, then once again, in earnest. "Hey, stop. Why are you upset? You go home tonight." He stopped talking, experiencing the cognitive process for the first time. Less than a month later he would quit his post.

Without the regularity of my job I began to sleep more frequently. It started innocent, a nap before lunch. Then it began infecting the whole day. I stopped going to breakfast, and skipped lunch twice, three times a week. Over time I realized it was happening again. Depression is a weird thing. For me, after the intense emotions subsided from losing the trial through sentencing, they were replaced by the new emotions that came with CRC and WCI; fear, mostly. Just after I was fired from my job I really had the time to appreciate how unhappy I had become. All of the intense emotions in their wake, left sentiments of apathy, it left whole beaches of extreme displeasure. I would stay up at night cycling the questions of my universe in my mind. Would I get out? When would I get out? Will I be home in six months? Will I be home in a year? Thirty years? The questions cycled endlessly in my mind. Too loud to go to sleep, and too quiet for anyone else to bare. I tried my best to keep my depression in, repressed. It was sad to think that my parents could still detect it. They could still hear the questions on my breath when we talked. What are my odds? Am I going to be free? I have to be free, right? Right? I tried to quiet the endless questions with work. I charted my general wellbeing: visits, calls, fatigue, happiness, hope, stress, etc... Through the data I attempted to find my optimum productivity. I scheduled my days down to the sleep and wake. Through it I wrote my first book. A short, insignificant novel about a man who completely lost his mind. It wasn't enough work. I read hundreds of pages, learned French, worked toward learning Russian, worked toward learning Japanese, outlined another book, then another, until I had reached a half dozen. Seven. Eight. I became obsessed with productivity to mass the depression that haunted me. I broke huge projects into four, six, eight and twelve week schedules. Each week got harder and each week I forgot more and more frequently about my depression. The only time I would remember was at night when the questions would creep back into my mind. Periodically Reuben would get me out of the cell to hang out in the day room.

Days stretched into weeks. I eventually answered an advertisement looking for tutors in the education building. After just three days I received a pass for training. There were fifteen guys in my class on the first day. But the last day three had left. We learned fundamentals of teaching phonics to algebra. Through working at the school we were told that we would need to teach students of all levels of education. A week after the course had ended we each were called back to the education building. The principal told us that we had all been hired and could request the classes we would like to be placed in. I said that I wanted to be in the literacy class, the lowest class that students could be placed into. I yearned for the opportunity to help people again and I had the image of myself as Adrien Brody teaching guys to enjoy education. Almost immediately we started work. Most of the time at work I was left doing nothing. So I read my newspaper and assisted two to three guys per day. Some needed help with a problem or two, and some were regulars. One was learning basic math, another pre-algebra. I enjoyed the challenge of working through a problem with them, finding out what exactly they didn't understand and forming it in a way that they could relate to. Fractions, for example, could always be brought to drugs as an example. A guy who has never been to a day of high school in his life can still relate to the euphemisms of drugs. Another of the benefits was the teacher for whom I worked. He spent sixteen years in China as a teacher where he met his wife. He was an altruist and the ultimate symbol of human endurance to me for bringing himself in every day to teach a group of state prisoners, many of whom didn't want to learn. He was one of the few humans that I met and I am extremely grateful for the opportunity. And then there were the days off. Being a school, at the end of each quarter we had several weeks of paid vacation before the next started. The first I experienced was spring break.

Reuben had pressed me for when my birthday was since around the time we initially met. I never told him, but two weeks before my birthday he found out. I insisted that I didn't want him to do anything, I just wanted it to be another day. He conceded, I thought until the day of April 1st. I had a visit and avoided any mention of birthdays around the dayroom in case anyone else found out. When it came time for my visit I showered, shaved, and walked out. I've always been conscious of how fleeting time is at a visit. It seems Linklater was right. Either I'm moving fast, or time is. Never simultaneously. While I was in the block I would be all over the place doing everything I could while time dragged on. As soon as I sat with my family time would speed by faster than I can believe. Before I knew it I was standing back outside of the visiting building, watching my family leave out the front gate, across the parking lot to their car and drive back off to another world.

I walked back to the block slowly and deliberately. Nineteen. I spent my first birthday in prison. How many more would there be? Would my appeal persuade the judges to a single ineffable truth, that I was innocent? Or, would history repeat itself? Ah, the unknowing of that time was the hardest part. Doubt seeped into every crevice and crack of my life until after an eternity I was finally standing once again at the door to my block. 1-A. One-Alpha. I enjoyed the silence for another second then opened the floodgate to the sound beyond. My friend Mark beckoned me too a table. He was acting strange, too strange. Suddenly, Reuben appeared from behind me with a tray filled with bowls. He made a cake, he made cookies, he made bowls of food, he even made a card. My birthday had not quite alluded me. I celebrated with my family and then I celebrated with my second family. Not bonded by blood, but by the iron shackles we all wore. We were fighting in the trenches. In a war zone without training, support or supply. The wire brought us together. Those damn fences brought me to the best friends I have ever known.

Give In

It so often occurred spontaneously. Je seraient lambiner throughout the day and then in its dark silent wake I would find myself weaving and occasionally floundering on the same white papyrus that even now I spin with a light blue Bic medium round stick - the instrument of my affair. Upon occasion I would find myself either laboring long into the night with one, two, three or even five thousand words. They would seem to flow from my subconscious through my ball point. Hardly ever have I found myself aware of the dictation of subtle cognition. This led me more times than one going on and on and on meaninglessly about this or that with absolutely no regard for consistency or coherency. And, then at times I would stare at my outlines and blank paper for days and weeks pondering how to continue without risking reading as more of a pompous oaf than is absolutely necessary. The former was a case when my dear brother, Alec, went to Europe. The latter is the case with these words. Each taking several minutes to conjugate into proper combinations of English alphabet characters. My brother's Europe trip was an interesting time for me as well. I had to deal with the consideration that my brother for the first time had left the country without me. Since I was eight years old I had not gone two years without leaving the country or one without boarding an airplane. My brother was traveling with friends to experience the wonders of the Eurozone. I suppose my melancholy is likely what fueled my long writing streak. At the time this particular project was set aside to finish a humorous piece about a man meeting himself. For the roughly five weeks my brother was abroad I kept on a strict schedule of between eight and twelve thousand words a week. On days that I wasn't writing I was reading, learning. I couldn't help but think that I was preparing myself. I wasn't and am still not wholly sure what I was preparing for but I worked myself harder than I had previously considered possible. Periodically my streak would be broken by a piece of correspondence from my brother giving updates and bits of news related to his trip. In those days of glimmering information I broke my concentration and would miss my day of work. By the end of his trip, the story of the man was completed and sent to him for typing. My first novel was completed. Weeks after approximately four months after submitting my appeal for consideration and ten months after entering County as a convicted murderer the appellate courts placed my case on the schedule for consideration. The date was July 14. From what I would surmise at this point the clerks that work for the judges had completed the research regarding my appeal as well as the prosecutor's response and had informed the judges of their findings. At this point the judges would deliberate on the 14th and we would hear an answer that day. I considered the three weeks that I was about to experience as extremely stressful. Though I wasn't yet concerned. As the days began to drag on I felt my capacity for work dwindling. Each day I did a little less. By the weekend I was hardly sleeping. I stayed up at night and stared out the open window tasting the fresh night air and wondering what my future would hold and I began the supposed last steps in the justice system. Within two days of learning the supposed deliberation of my fate I was living nearly void of sleep. I had come so far and now the light I saw could be that of my freedom. My confidence in all my projects dwindled to nothing and over the next few weeks my average words wrote per day went from 1428 to just under 200, my average happiness plummeted from 7-8 to 2-4, my stress went from 4-5 to 8-10, my sleep erratically shifted from nonexistent to binge sleeping. Relationships with my friends dwindled, my faith faltered and I hardly ever showed up to work.

On the Saturday before the day of reckoning I learned that the day of deliberation did not mean that they would post their opinion. In fact, it usually took between two and eight weeks after their meeting before posting their findings. So now not only was I stressed about leaving or staying, I was angry that it was taking so long to complete the process. The next days were drenched with apathy. I showed up to work and tutored those I could, I called my family and neglected to make adequate conversation and I avoided contact with anyone that I could. When that Tuesday came I received a pass to pick up mail from the package room for the next day.
Walking down the road on Wednesday it was easy to be excited. I hadn't expected anything, though *Go Set A Watchman* by Harper Lee had been released the day before. Sure enough when I arrived at the package room

the blue binding was slid across the divider to me. My mother was elated that her surprise duped me for the most part. I dove; gracefully delicately ethereal, silently and determined head long into the pages of my beloved Ms. Lee. Ten months in the past I could recall acutely the exact details of *Mockingbird*. Every word of her beauty echoed in my mind. The profound theme of disillusionment stuck out to me and touched me on a surreal level. The dichotomy that first stuck out to me in Atticus Finch was quickly cast aside. He had hardly changed. His concern throughout both novels was that of the Law and the wellbeing of Scout. He knew that he couldn't be God to her forever, he had to be humanized. His thoughts pertaining towards racial issues was not incorrect, just relevant to the time period. It was beautiful. And it forced me to take a serious look at myself in this phase of my life. I was balancing precariously between being an adult and a child. When I looked at myself in the mirror I could see the grey area between the child and adult wearing all over me. My eyes were that of an adult, a man at the beginning of his life, wise and ready for the world. My lip showed the maturity of a 17 year old. My face began to wear like that of an old man. I was looking through adult eyes at a child's body that was still growing. The Catholic instruction class I took spoke often on the cusp of manhood and my teacher noted on my take home work that I was matured beyond my age. The class came closer and closer to me and I began to seek a stronger faith with God again. For the first time alone in my cell one day I knelt on the cement with the rosary I received in class and recited it. When I had finished I asked for strength to continue on, protection for my family, friends, enemies, CO's and that I would have the strength to...
"Hey, what are you doing?" I opened my eyes and saw Reuben standing at the door.

"Hmm? oh, I'm just praying." He laughed and stepped in.

"I can see that, dork. Are you praying the rosary like we did in class?"

I shook my head. "Sort of. I did it a lot when I was in elementary school in class so I'm doing it like we did there. It's a lot alike though."

"Do you need me to leave?"
"No, it's almost-oh wow it's time to go to Toastmasters." I stood up and grabbed my folder.

"Do you have your speech ready?"

I laughed. "Well.... What does it need to be on?" I picked up my pen.
"It's just a 5 minute intro on me. It shouldn't be hard, I don't think."

"Well, good luck." He said. I walked out of our cell and out the door of the block. The sun had begun to set and was setting the sky ablaze. Clouds were clustered around the setting orb, turning the sky into a spectrum of hues. I left just before the yard opened and inmates were allowed to walk on the roads so I was the only one walking on the road toward the education building where Toastmasters was held. Toastmasters is a public speaking organization that had been started by a guy named Michael who had been incarcerated for twenty four years. It's an organization on the streets and he had brought it into prison. I kept running the first words I wanted to say through my head.

"Mr. Toastmaster, fellow toastmasters and distinguished guests: My name is Patrick McGail and today I will be giving my icebreaker speech." All the way into the building I muttered it to myself, once I got into the room I started repeating it over and over again in my head. Once the meeting started I felt my nerves building up. I started to tell myself over and over to just calm down and talk slow. Before I knew it I was walking to the front of the room towards the Toastmaster, Gill. I shook his hand and turned to the audience with a smile.

"Mr. Toastmaster, fellow toastmasters and distinguished guests: My name is… My name is Patrick McGail and I am here today to give my Icebreaker speech. {**Relax, One. Two. Three.**} If you remember a month or so ago I stood up here and told you a little bit about myself. Today I would like to elaborate on it…as I said then I am here for twenty four years to life for murder, aggravated robbery and aggravated burglary. {**One. Two. Three. Breath.**} Before I caught my case I had just graduated a year early from high school and was taking a few general education courses to prepare for college. I wasn't really sure what I wanted to do yet, I had considered majoring in psychology but I had also considered majoring in English literature. I didn't know what exactly I wanted to do, but hey, I had time to figure it out. {**Make eye contact. Keep it slow.**} Once I caught my case I completely fell off of everything I had been doing. {**Integrate the words of the day, stop moving your hands like that, you look weird.**} I lost all of my momentum because even though I had MOTIVATION I didn't have PERSEVERANCE. I had never been dragged through the mud before so I didn't know how to pick myself back up. My Dad sent me a letter a few weeks into my stay and I'll always remember what he said. He told me to *Stay you.* That hit home more than anything else. He said that *Although what you are going through is really rough, we will do our part and fight to get you out, but you need to do your part and stay you.* He was telling me that whatever happens was going to happen. I needed to keep doing the things that I did best. Now, a year and ten

months after I first caught my case and nearly a year into my immuring, I've kept doing what he told me to do, and now I see the quality of what he was saying. When I was in school I had motivation but no perseverance. By telling me to stay me he was teaching me perseverance. Since while I have been here at WCI I primarily do three things. Write, read, and learn."
{**Slow down. Breath.**} Based on my average of words written per day I have written one hundred and ninety two thousand words since coming to Warren Correctional. I currently have nineteen writing projects that I am working on. Most of what I read is the *Wall Street Journal* but I also enjoy Nabokov, Lee and Fitzgerald. When I read I like to pay careful attention to their writing styles including framework, subtle details and recurring vocabulary. I learn a lot from reading authors such as them. {**How am I doing on time? Two minutes? okay.**} I also have been working to learn French, Russian and Japanese. I have learned a significant amount on French but unfortunately I haven't gotten very far in the other two.
{**You're rambling, wrap it up.**} I feel blessed through all of the hardships I have gone through. Although what I am going through is rough I know that it could have been a lot worse. I was sent to a camp that isn't very hard and was granted the opportunity to learn which I know that elsewhere would have been impossible. For that I am very thankful and I know that God is watching over me closely. Thank you all for listening and I look forward to working with you all. Mr. Toastmaster?"

Even now I remember how relieved I was to be done with that speech. That was last Wednesday. Today is Friday the fourteenth of August. It's been exactly one year since the verdict was rendered in my trial. I've been in prison or jail for a year. 365 days. That's 1095 meals. 8760 hours. 31,536,000 seconds. It's been a long ride. It's been four weeks since the appeals court discussed my case. Last Friday they rendered decisions on all but mine and one other. Today or next Friday I will likely hear what my fate is. I've been scared every deadline since my verdict and every Friday since they discussed my case. Except today. Today I'm just excited for my visit this evening. I'm not thinking about judges or the law but my family and the next time I see them. I've surrendered myself. Either way, whether I get out or not, my life will still be worth living. If I get out then I will be elated. If I stay then I will keep writing and just keep living. My life will not stop because of the decision of dusty old men. nor is my freedom based on the proximity of the wire. Whether I'm here or in California or on a cruise ship my freedom depends solely on me. It depends on how much control I decide to have in my life. If I'm here I can choose to be happy, though if I'm pushing a pencil behind a desk I am out sourcing that decision to the corporate sector. I would like to thank you for reading the story of this part of my life and no matter what happens in your life, just

Staying Me

stay you.

Epilog

It wasn't long after finishing the last chapter that I realized the truth. The appeal court denied my petition on all accounts except a sentencing detail, which, when I returned to court for resolution ended up with me having the same amount of time as before plus five years post-release control. It was an interesting situation to return to county. I immediately remembered the setting of the first scene of this book and now, after reading this book for the first time since hand writing it, I have to admit that I want to change every detail. I want to change the way that I perceived this place at first, The way I reacted to certain situations, the way that I have at times talked to the family that has supported me endlessly. I especially want to change the first words of the book. I would give anything to not have come into prison, to be looking at 24, 22 years now, to life in prison at just twenty. I can't say that I could have done much different to foresee this situation evolving in the way it did and completely avoiding it, but I guess that is life. I suppose that it's just as impossible to change what led me to trial as it would be to rewrite the words in this book. I can't change the past, nobody can. I just have the luxury of re-reading it and re-experiencing it in intense detail. I have changed all the names of the individuals in this book and changed certain distinguishing factors to protect the individuals portrayed within. Everything else within this book is true and accurate. Even now, on September 12, 2016, I find myself wishing myself away. Even after everything I have been through and everything I have said I still wish this never would have happened. I would give everything to be able to stop the disastrous mistakes that led the individuals who committed the crime I'm doing time for, and I will always be torn with guilt that I can never do anything to make it better or change what happened. I pray for guidance. I pray that the words of this book can help someone somewhere prevent this kind of atrocity from happening again. I pray for the ability to reach those whose lives I can suade in the right directions so that they don't have to watch life from behind glass waiting their turn for a truncated experience. I pray for peace and serenity for families of violent crimes, families of the convicted who have lost pieces of themselves, and the individuals who one day will have an opportunity to rejoin society. I pray that my friends and family can still lead full, happy lives even after what these events have done to them and I pray for guidance and protection for those who claim to be my enemies, that they will find peace in their lives. I don't want to put out a book that is simply a complaint about how horrible my situation is. I want to just provide a way for others to see inside this system and realize how terribly wrong it's working. The guilty are not receiving treatment so one day they return to society. They are returning as the exact same criminals. The system needs to be changed so that the people rejoining society are educated leaders who can pull our communities up from the ashes and stop the younger generation before they travel down the same road. Please, I pray that you will take my words and live your life considering the consequences of your actions and the actions of those you associate as if they may affect rest of your life. Because one day, they might. I love you all and thank you so much for reading my book, Staying Me.

ABOUT THE AUTHOR

Patrick McGail has written two other books, T*he Life and Works of Louis Vettin* and *Trois Idées*. He is Vice President of his Toastmasters club, a student at Adams State University pursuing an MBA, and the founder of an inmate based company which provides business newsletters, Omega Prime Financials.

Patrick is currently imprisoned for murder, a crime to which he maintains his innocence, and is scheduled for the parole board in 2038.

Patrick is a devout Catholic and aspires one day to give motivational speeches to at-risk youth about turning their lives around.

www.ingramcontent.com/pod-product-compliance
Lightning Source LLC
Chambersburg PA
CBHW070318190526
45169CB00005B/1660